Rooted in Love

Integrating Ignatian spirituality into daily life

First published in South Africa, 2013
by New Voices Publishing
www.newvoices.co.za

First edition September 2013, in paperback & ebook

ISBN for PRINT: 978-0-620-57861-5

ISBN for EBOOK: 978-0-620-57862-2

cover photograph: Hannes Thiart

Rooted in Love

Integrating Ignatian spirituality into daily life

Margaret A.L. Blackie

With a foreword by Margaret Silf

One of the greatest challenges of reading this soon-to-be-published book by Margaret Blackie is that I can't yet give this volume to everyone I know. In a world with no shortage of Ignatian titles, *Rooted in Love* forges through brilliant new territory with profound grace.

This book is at once practical and deeply spiritual. Using quotes from poet Mary Oliver, citing all manner of written works, and prompts that ask one to look inward and outward, Blackie has given us a gift of a book. I would recommend *Rooted in Love* to anyone with an interest exploring Ignatian spirituality, and I would recommend it as well to those already deeply living the Spiritual Exercises.

Clear, thoughtful, practical, and wise. *Rooted in Love* is destined to be the "go-to" book for many on the spiritual path – and for good reason.

— *Fran Rossi Szpylczyn*, Catholic speaker, writer and lay minister blogging at *There Will Be Bread*

Margaret Blackie has written with elegance and grace from her intimate knowledge of the landscape of the spiritual life, both as an honest practitioner and as a spiritual director. I warmly recommend this book for both beginners and those further along the path that Saint Ignatius has mapped for us. For while many have made the pilgrimage before us, we do well to have Margaret with us as an accomplished guide. You will treasure walking next to her.

— *Tim Muldoon*, author of *The Ignatian Workout* and *The Ignatian Workout for Lent*.

Mags Blackie's introduction to Ignatian spirituality is a book I wanted to keep putting down -- so I could spend time with the practical exercises she threads throughout the text; so I could linger with the poets she pulls in; so I could notice the ways in which God was at work with me. Blackie wonderfully weaves her own experiences as both a spiritual director and a pilgrim in this world into her cogent and welcoming explanations of the foundations of Saint Ignatius' way of being in the world.

—*Michelle Francl Donnay,* blogger and academic

When I skim through some books, I soon replace them feeling I've already gleaned their message. That's not the case with *Rooted in Love* where every page is richly practical yet full of the wonderful hope that we can truly live in the reality of God's love. This book will be my faith companion for many months to come.

— *Tracy Williamson,* Christian author and speaker

Mags Blackie is a credible witness to a life *Rooted in Love.* With generosity and profound insight, she explores how the deep treasures of Ignatian spirituality shed light on our journey into the heart of God. Through her wisdom, born of her own intensely reflective faith-experience, she becomes our trusted guide and companion along the Way. I warmly commend this book to anyone who wants to bring their everyday life and faith in God together in more life-giving way.

— *Trevor Hudson,* Methodist minister and author

Margaret Blackie has done a wonderful service to readers by distilling the essentials of Ignatian spirituality into a short and reader-friendly book. With great humility she shares her own experience of how this spirituality has helped her to develop a deep and meaningful relationship with God. Readers will find her a compassionate and down-to-earth guide to developing their own relationship with God and thus finding more meaning in their lives. I recommend this book.

—*William A. Barry SJ,* author of many books on Ignatian spirituality and spiritual direction

To my mum and dad, Adrienne and Fergus.

Acknowledgements

This book emerges from fifteen years of immersion in Ignatian spirituality. Along the way there have been many valuable encounters. One of the most precious spaces has been the giving and receiving of spiritual direction. I cannot thank by name those who have shared their journeys with me, but I am deeply grateful for all I have learnt and witnessed in being allowed to enter this sacred space. To my own directors over the years: I am deeply grateful for your prayerful attendance to my being.

There are a few individuals to whom I am particularly grateful. Without their assistance and companionship this book might never have come into being:

The team at Loyola Hall, Jesuit Spirituality Centre in Merseyside, UK, who invited me to join them in both the work and living in community for four years.

Ruth Holgate, Rob Marsh SJ and Paul Nicholson SJ with whom I had many vibrant conversations on the minutiae of Ignatian spirituality and spiritual direction.

Dermot Preston SJ who directed me through the *Spiritual Exercises* and opened the world of Ignatian spirituality to me.

Nan Martin, for facilitating my initial foray into spiritual direction and for companionship in these last few years.

Denise Ackermann, Judy Cannan, Elsabe O'Leary, Ron Perry SJ and Margaret Silf, for feedback on the manuscript; the book is better for your comments.

Biddy Greene, for your painstaking editing and being willing to push me even when I was most resistant.

Cal Blackie and Phil Starks for providing a sanctuary in which most of the book was written and for conversations on some of the themes.

Vicky Hindmarch, who kept body and soul together with acupuncture and walks on the Mountain.

Delia Saunderson and Felicity Harrison for being my unwavering support throughout the process.

Margaret Silf for tremendous encouragement in the process of writing, and for her generous words in the Foreword, and most importantly, for being willing to allow her name to be associated with this book.

Mags Blackie
Cape Town, 31 July 2013

Contents

Foreword

You are invited to take a walk with a guide who loves to hike and who knows the hidden twists and turns, the hazards and the unexpected viewpoints, along the way. The terrain you will cover will be the landscape of Ignatian spirituality, and your walk will be a spiritual journey. The route you will take will follow closely the dynamic first explored five hundred years ago by a man from the Basque country of Spain, called Inigo, later to become St Ignatius Loyola, who has since become a beloved guide to many Christians of all traditions. There is no shortage of books explicating this dynamic. There is, however, a significant lack of books that make the journey truly accessible to ordinary travellers. The book you are holding goes a long way to address that lack.

There is a mountainous region of England called The Lake District. There are many guidebooks to the Lake District, but the outstanding and best-loved set of guides was produced by a man called Alfred Wainwright who was a civil servant who spent all his free time roaming these hills. His guides are the fruit of his own experience, and describe in compelling detail the features along the way, every hidden crevice, every summit cairn. He illustrates each hike with detailed sketches and friendly warnings and encouragements. As you read, and follow his routes, you not only *see* the path, but you can almost smell it, feel it, taste it. Margaret Blackie offers you here a guide to the spiritual journey written in the same spirit as Wainwright's. You could have no better guide. She knows this journey intimately – because she walks it herself with passionate engagement – while also being well aware that for every traveller the way will be unique.

What will this journey ask of you? Well, some courage is required if you are going to risk this adventure into the deeper reaches of your being. As you walk, you will encounter the power of your own desires, and learn to sift those that are life-giving from those that are not. You will also stumble into what the author describes as 'fault-lines' in your personal landscape – issues that trigger pain in you or set alarm bells ringing, maybe because they activate old memories or future fears. But above all you will catch glimpses of a beauty and a love beyond your wildest imagining. So the journey asks you to walk with the eyes of your heart wide open to mystery. Don't be afraid: you are not walking alone. Both you and your guide are accompanied every step of the way by the one who describes himself as 'the way, the truth and the life.'

And where will your journey lead? We naturally assume that any journey must lead to a destination. The spiritual journey is different. It's not so much about arriving at a destination, as about discovering a *destiny*. In fact, if you think you have arrived, you have probably got stuck in a cul-de-sac. So what is this destiny towards which you strive? Nothing less than becoming who you truly are – the uniquely precious and beloved person you are created to be. The goal is already within you. This book will help you to grow into it in your own personal way.

Travel joyfully, and enjoy the walk!

Margaret Silf, July 2013

Introduction

In early 2012, I was giving spiritual direction to a person who had been through a very difficult period but had worked through their pain, confusion and internal chaos. There was a sense of Spring in the conversation, of life beginning to emerge from an emotional wintertime, and an image began to develop in my mind – of a small shrub held in the soil; held in the hands of God. The shrub symbolised the person's life, and the soil their life experience. The soil was composted with processed life experience. The detritus of pain, confusion and chaos had been broken down into something which now nourished the plant.

What struck me most forcibly about the image was that the more that life experience is processed, grappled with and understood, the richer the soil becomes – and the greater the strength of the shrub, the more beautiful its flowers and the more plentiful its fruit. The beauty and the plenty do not arise from the shrub *doing* anything, but come simply from its *being*.

I know that this image has been very helpful to the person who was with me in spiritual direction that day. And it has spoken profoundly to me as well. In simply living each day and getting on with the tasks associated with my life, I am fulfilling what I am called to. I can say this because I believe that my work both as an academic chemist and as a spiritual director, as well as my social life and my family all contribute to my way of being in the world – and that this way of being in the world is what I am called to right now. So, in a very tangible way, I do feel that, in simply living my life, I am fulfilling my vocation. The achievements which come along the way are an important part of the process, but if I can focus on living each day and doing what needs to be done each day, the products will take care of themselves in due course. My life will be measured by my attendance to each day, by my attendance to *being* – not by the pile of products.

It is important to notice though that life experience must be continually reflected upon and processed in some way. Time by itself may diminish the intensity of an experience, but it is only when it is worked through that experience can become nourishment for the soul.

But we live in a world which favours the numbing of life experience over grappling with it. Brené Brown describes this 'numbing behaviour' in her book *The Gifts of Imperfection:*[1]

> When we talked about how they dealt with difficult emotions (such as shame, grief, fear, despair, disappointment, and sadness), I heard over and over about the need to numb and take the edge off the feelings that cause vulnerability, discomfort, and pain. Participants described engaging in behaviours that numbed their feelings or helped them to avoid experiencing pain. Some of these participants were fully aware that their behaviour had a numbing effect, while others did not make the connection. When I interviewed the participants whom I'd describe as living a Wholehearted life about the same topic, they consistently talked about *trying to feel the feelings, staying mindful about numbing behaviours, and trying to lean into the discomfort of hard emotions.*

We do need to numb our experience to some extent. Engaging in healthy numbing behaviour such as exercise or creative work or light conversation is an important part of

---

1   Brené Brown (2010) p.69. (See References for full details of works cited in the footnotes.)

grappling with life experience, but it is crucial that we recognise this for what it is. Work itself can be healthy numbing behaviour if it affords us the luxury of focusing on the task at hand. If we are able to live the kind of 'Wholehearted life' described by Brené Brown, we will be well on our way to being able to live in the present, and to truly savour the gifts of the present. This way of living allows us a glimpse of the truth that the value we have as people comes from our way of *being* in the world, not from what we *do*. This is not to say, that in simply 'being' we will not be fruitful or productive, but rather that if we can focus on the being, then the fruit really will take care of itself. It is not the fruit that gives our lives meaning – our lives are much more than simply what we produce. In our world today, this is a truth that is sometimes hard to hold on to.

The image I have shared here is deeply meaningful to me because it marks the moment when I began to truly grasp that simply *being* is enough. I had caught glimpses of this truth before, but I was so busy trying to make myself acceptable to the people around me that I could not hold it. I had had the *feeling* of being in the right place, but what shifted for me was the *sufficiency* of being in the right place. In that image, I discovered that simply by being myself I am fulfilling my purpose. By living my life as it is today, with the ups and downs, the moments of great insight and the moments of petty rivalry, I am living my vocation. I am doing exactly what I have been called to do.

It sounds so extraordinarily simple, and in some ways it is. I have found it a relief to realise that I need not complete some great task to make myself loveable or acceptable. Nonetheless, this 'simply being' comes with some fine print. I know that it is in my nature to teach and to write. So, to be fully myself, I have to do both of these things in some measure. I cannot be myself fully without taking time to know myself. I must face my pain. I must examine my failures. I must celebrate my successes. I must also live in the world, developing and nurturing substantial relationships within my world.

The purpose of this book is, then, to provide something of a guide for the kind of exploration that I have found useful. It is essentially a collection of thoughts and ideas. Over the last fifteen years, Ignatian spirituality has slowly seeped into and permeated my being. It has become the framework that I use to interpret both my own experience and the experiences of those who have chosen to share their spiritual journeys with me.

I have spent most of my adult life searching for my place in the world. In recent years I have found a niche where I seem to fit, at least for the moment. Now that I have found this place, I feel that I can share some of the tools that have helped me thus far. So I write this particular book at this particular time because I have been ruminating over these things for long enough. In observing my own journey in these years, I realise that there will be many twists and turns in the road ahead, and that I would not write the same book in five years' time. I offer this now as a way of thinking, a way of praying, a way of being – precisely because this is my way of thinking and praying and being at this moment. It is a gift I have now, and I do not want to waste it by waiting for 'a better time'.

This book offers a way into a life of purpose, a life with God. It is not the only way, and it may not work well for everyone. In the process of writing about faith and grace, I have become very aware of the particularity of my own experience. Your brain and your reflective processes will operate quite differently from mine. So you may be tempted, on occasion, to dismiss a specific idea simply because the experience, as I describe it, is unfamiliar to you. Nonetheless, I have heard many others describe their experiences and, whilst the detail is obviously different, there is always something common in the essence of these encounters. So my advice is to read the detail lightly, and in the end pause and notice whether there is any whisper of resonance in your own life.

Some background and context

In any bookshop you will find a large section devoted to helping people make their lives better. In one sense the material in this book is no different. It is about learning to make choices intentionally. It is about learning to notice and pay attention to the movements that happen within you as you engage in various aspects of your life. I describe here a way in which you can examine your motivations and notice your desires. It is this observation and reflection which will begin to reveal to you the differences between those things that are truly life-giving and those which merely look appealing.

The book is also about the importance of developing relationships. It is fundamentally a Christian book, so your relationship with God is a central theme. It is important to recognise from the outset that this central relationship is also supported and nourished by your relationships with those around you. It is impossible to engage seriously in deepening relationship with God without deepening your relationship with others. It is also impossible to do either of those things without coming to know yourself better in the process. So in a very real sense this book is not about self-help. It is about engaging more in community, engaging more in family, paying attention to what happens when one does that, and allowing oneself to be transformed in the process.

The fundamental ideas are drawn explicitly and unashamedly from *The Spiritual Exercises of St Ignatius*. This book, a true gem, was first published in 1548. In the almost five hundred years since then, it has provided a framework for spiritual growth and development for many people. Some of the more notable examples are Francis Xavier – one of the early Jesuit companions who headed off to the East, stopping for some years in India and then trying to reach China; Edmund Campion – a Catholic martyr of Tudor England; Mary Ward – the seventeenth century English founder of the Institute of the Blessed Virgin Mary who was held under house arrest for daring to found an apostolic order for women, and Pedro Arrupe – a loved and respected Jesuit Superior General for many years, who was in Hiroshima in August 1945. But a word of caution: *The Spiritual Exercises* is not a book to be simply read by anyone. It is a manual intended for the spiritual director. It outlines a series of exercises to be given by a director, and prayed through by the 'exercitant'.[2]

The Spiritual Exercises comes from a distillation of the experiences of Ignatius of Loyola. Ignatius is probably best known as the founder of the Jesuit order, but he has had a far more extensive impact on Roman Catholic spirituality than may be immediately evident. Indeed in the last century that impact has been felt right across the Christian world – in part because the Ignatian tradition is the foundation for the vast majority of spiritual direction courses. I use *The Spiritual Exercises* as the foundation of much of what I write here for two reasons. Firstly, because I have found that *The Spiritual Exercises* and Ignatian spirituality have given me a language in which to describe my internal landscape. I first encountered Ignatian spirituality in my early twenties. I have been immersed in it for much of my adult life, and it has been the framework I have used as I have grown and developed. I think now that it is a good fit for my particular personality, and the time investment gives a depth and resonance which I find enormously helpful. Secondly, it is a spirituality which is founded on the principle of 'finding God in all things'. It is a spirituality intended for adaptation (or application) to one's daily life – regardless of what that life actually looks like. So it requires no major deviation from regular life in order to immerse oneself fully in this spirituality.

Ignatian spirituality thus has much to offer to all who seek a deeper relationship with God. Where other spiritual traditions, like the Benedictine tradition for example, require adherence to a very particular pattern and rhythm of prayer,

2   'Exercitant' is the term given to a person who is making the Spiritual Exercises.

Ignatian spirituality has no such requirement. More importantly, Ignatius expected that we would find God in all of our daily activities, not just in the ones that appear to be 'holy' or intentionally directed towards God. Ignatius himself went through a period of being 'tempted by prayer'. While he was studying in Paris he found himself frequently extending his allotted time of prayer, giving up sleep and neglecting his studies in order to pray. After a time, however, he realised that failing to follow through on his studies would not achieve the greater good of being able to preach. He realised that he was indulging his desire for consolation at the expense of helping others encounter God. He did not, of course, abandon prayer altogether: he simply stuck to the time he had allocated to prayer, trusting that God could do whatever it was that God needed to do in the given time.

So Ignatian spirituality is then a spirituality designed to be lived in the midst of life. Of course, periodic withdrawal is good – in fact even necessary – but, for the ordinary person, Ignatian spirituality needs no life adaptation.

The Weeks of the Spiritual Exercises

Before going any further it will probably be useful for me to explain a few things about *The Spiritual Exercises*. As I have already said, it is not a book to be read, but rather a guide for the spiritual director. The Exercises are designed to be made as a thirty day silent retreat, although there are other ways of making the full Exercises.

The Exercises are divided into four Weeks. It is important to understand that the term 'Week' does not mean a period of seven days; it is better to think of the Weeks as four periods of time. Each Week has a specific dynamic, and each Week is characterised by a particular 'grace'.

- The First Week is intended for everyone. It comprises, for each person, the experience of discovering two things: I am truly, deeply loved by God; and I am flawed and broken. The grace of the First Week is to know that I am a loved sinner.

- The Second Week encompasses the life of Jesus from the Incarnation up until the entry into Jerusalem on Palm Sunday. The grace of the Second Week is my getting to know Jesus as a person – often expressed in terms of the prayer of Richard of Chichester 'to see thee more clearly, to love thee more dearly, to follow thee more nearly'. The Second Week is about developing a sense of companionship with Jesus so that I can explore the ways in which Jesus' companionship is manifest in my daily life.

- The Third Week covers the period from Palm Sunday to the death of Jesus. The grace here is to feel sorrow with Christ in sorrow. That is, to be a companion of Jesus even through his Passion. It has the dual purpose of recognising the full implications of my companionship with Jesus and, conversely, beginning to see Jesus' companionship in my experiences of suffering.

- The Fourth Week begins with the Resurrection. The grace of the Fourth Week is to feel joy with Christ in joy. This gives me access to an experience of redemption, suggesting that, even in the midst of chaos, a small seed of hope can take root and grow. Redeeming grace can bring good out of the worst, the bleakest of situations.

In some ways it is the juxtaposition of the Third and Fourth Weeks of the Spiritual Exercises which are held in the image at the beginning of this chapter. With the compost of grace, new life can emerge from the detritus of suffering.

A few words about me

In the years that I have worked and taught in spirituality I have found the most natural way to explain a point is to take an example from my own life. As a result, some parts of this book contain autobiographical illustrations. I think this adds a certain richness to the text, although I am well aware that my world view has of course been shaped my own life experiences. So, to reveal some of those lenses, I should add a few words about myself.

I am an academic and my field of expertise is chemistry. I work at Stellenbosch University, in a town nestled between vineyards and mountains in the beautiful Western Cape of South Africa. I am the last of five children and I am single. I come from a highly educated family (all of us have at least one postgraduate degree) and my abiding memory of childhood is having conversations around the breakfast table on Sunday mornings. I am a practising Roman Catholic. I have explored other Christian traditions and I work closely with those from other traditions. Although I struggle with some aspects of the Church, the understanding of the Eucharist fuels my faith in a fundamental way, and ultimately the graces outweigh the difficulties for me – and so I remain within the Church. I worked in England as a full time spiritual director for four years, from 2003 to 2006, and I still give spiritual direction and train people as spiritual directors. As a Zimbabwean, I live with the loss of the place that was my home. My friends and family are scattered across the globe. I have lived in four countries in Africa and Europe but my sanctuary is with my sister in Massachusetts.

One of the recurring themes in this book is a call to honesty: Honesty with oneself, honesty with God, honesty with others. This comes directly out of reflection on a very painful period in my own life. As I grappled with some of the challenges I faced and slowly found my way through, I discovered that the turning point on each issue was honesty: a willingness to face my real desire; my brokenness; my giftedness; my anger; my grief – in the presence of God. It is in this discovery that I find I am finally able to give voice to many of the ideas that I have carried for the last decade. It is perhaps because I have discovered that grace can flourish even when I am not strong that I dare to hold up my thoughts for inspection: not as one who knows, but as one who is dedicated to continuing to explore; not as one who is strong, but as one who has tasted the fruit of vulnerability.

A few words on the book

Key Ignatian themes permeate these pages. In some places I have found it a real challenge to translate the Ignatian terms into ordinary English usage, so I have tried to explain their real-world meaning with personal examples. In other places I have intentionally used terms which are not often part of regular conversation. Do not get caught too much on the words I use; feel the resonance and let that guide your reading. There is enormous value in these ideas.

You will find that some ideas and concepts are repeated through the book in different ways. This is because the path into greater depth of relationship with God is not a linear one. There are tools which can help along the way, but they are intertwined. There is some sense of order, some lessons naturally come before others, and our understanding develops and broadens over time. We begin to make connections with different facets of faith, and the bigger picture slowly takes shape. In writing the book I have of course been limited by the need to present things in some order, and I have chosen the order which makes most sense to me. Some of the ideas I use in earlier chapters are more fully developed only later on. I cannot find a way around this, and some of the experiences I use to illustrate different points are mentioned more than once. This is not an oversight, it is intentional.

This book is not simply a book to be read; I hope that it will, rather, provide a springboard into prayer. Within each chapter you will find invitations to pause, to reflect, to pray. Your reading of the book will be enriched if you take time to engage with these invitations; doing this will help you root the material of the chapter in your own experience. If you find elements of this book useful, it is most likely that these will be in those places where you have already found some kind of resonance, or where the description helps put words onto something which you have experienced but not yet named. Either way, giving time and space to consciously allow the connection to happen will be useful.

In Chapter 1, in particular, I have punctuated the prose with exercises. You will get more out of the book if you do these exercises. In later chapters I suggest that you pay attention to the inner promptings which emerge *as you read*. Keep a pen and paper with you as you read, or keep a note on your electronic device. As something strikes you, write it down. Use these jottings as grist to the mill of your daily prayer. The kind of prayer that will suit this most is conversational prayer – as Ignatius puts it: talking to God as one friend talks to another.

The contemporary translation, on the next page, of the Principle and Foundation from The Spiritual Exercises *provides the springboard into the book. This text is referred to several times in this book, and there is a full discussion of its meaning in Chapter 7.*

Principle and Foundation

The goal of our life is to live with God forever.
God, who loves us, gave us life.
Our own response of love allows God's life
to flow into us without limit.
All the things in this world are a gift of God,
presented to us so that we can know God more easily
and make a return of love more readily.
As a result, we appreciate and use all these gifts of God
insofar as they help us develop as loving persons.
But if any of these gifts become the centre of our lives,
they displace God
and so hinder our growth toward our goal.
In everyday life, then, we must hold ourselves in balance
before all of these created gifts insofar as we have a
choice
and are not bound by some obligation.
We should not fix our desires on health or sickness,
wealth or poverty, success or failure, a long life or a short
one.
For everything has the potential of calling forth in us
a deeper response to our life in God.
Our only desire and our one choice should be this:
I want and choose what better leads
to God's deepening his life in me.[3]

The *Principle and Foundation* is found at the beginning of **The Spiritual Exercises**. *Read through it a few times and notice what strikes you.*
Take some time to talk to God about that.

---

3   David Fleming (1993) p.9.

Chapter 1: Taking Stock

Listen, are you breathing just a little, and calling it a life?
— Mary Oliver

In this chapter I offer an invitation to stop and notice consciously what is going on in your life. I ask questions about your experience of aspects of the material that is to follow in the chapter. You will get more out of the chapter if you explicitly link your reading to your own experience. You are also likely to remember more of the material this way. John Dewey, the American pragmatist, philosopher and educationalist, argues strongly for the importance of linking education to personal experience. You will find these short sections in every chapter.

As mentioned in the Introduction, in this chapter in particular, you will also find exercises punctuating the text. These exercises should be done as prayer exercises. Either include them over a number of days in your daily prayer, or take the chapter and find somewhere you can be undisturbed for a few hours and slowly work your way through the chapter, stopping to pray whenever an exercise is given. The exercises begin with a fairly full description of what I am expecting you to be talking to God about.

This chapter helps you ask what is going on for you right now. What are you looking for? What is motivating you? Where is God? It is not a trivial starting point, a chapter to be quickly skimmed through before you get to the real meat. Take your time. The ways in which you chew, savour and digest the rest of the book will be strongly influenced by these factors.

In my experience it is only when we consciously stop and pay attention to different aspects of our daily reality that we begin to see the whole picture. As we rush through life, we do see glimpses of where we are, of where God is. But it is easy to take these impressions as being true to the whole; relying only on these glimpses is likely to give a distorted vision. The invitation here is to take some time to ponder; to view from different angles; to reflect. Ask God to show you what God wants you to see.

For the good stuff, offer thanks; for the not so good stuff, just hold it up before God and see what emerges. This contemplation will become an opportunity to shape your life – and to savour it.

Why you are reading this book?

What are you looking for from these pages? There are no right or wrong answers – what matters is the act of paying attention to the questions and noticing the thoughts that emerge. In doing this you will become more aware of the purpose of what you are doing.

This process of daring to ask why, daring to look at the purpose, is a fundamental component of Ignatian spirituality. Again, the actual answers do not matter. The 'bringing to consciousness' will help you become more aware of what is going on within your being. The act of noticing will, in time, lead to a deepening of your understanding of God, and of your relationship with God; a deepening of your understanding of others and your relationships with them; and a deepening understanding of yourself.

In what is in essence an overture to *The Spiritual Exercises*, Ignatius gives his Principle and Foundation. He lays out what he sees as the purpose of human life: the salvation of the soul. I find this idea easier to understand if I express purpose in terms of deepening relationship with God – essentially these amount to the same thing. In this paragraph Ignatius says that all things in life are there to help us towards the end of deepening our relationship with God.

There are two important points here. Firstly, we need to pay attention to the trajectory of our interactions. By this I mean that some things that are helpful to other people will not necessarily be as helpful for you, and vice versa. It is important to pay attention to how you feel after a cup of coffee with a friend, or reading a particular book, or magazine or website. To notice which things are truly edifying, as opposed to those things which are demeaning; to notice which things seem to resonate with the deepest sense of who you are, as opposed to those things which cause fragmentation or confusion.

It is then important to begin to practise actively choosing those things which are drawing out the best in you. This act of 'discernment' will be covered in much greater depth later on, but for now it is important to realise that not all things labelled 'church' or 'love', and so on will actually be edifying for you. In addition, some things will be fairly neutral, they will be enjoyable, but it is not clear that they have any particular purpose. It is useful to notice these things, because they can provide a wonderful (temporary) escape when things get tough. These are the things which help to numb the raw edge of reality.

Secondly, all things in life can lead us into deeper relationship with God. We do not have to focus only on the 'religious' stuff. A phrase often repeated in Ignatian circles is 'finding God in all things'. It is important that we pay attention to the presence of God in our daily lives: a chance conversation which leaves us feeling uplifted; a beautiful sunset; sublime music; a poem which speaks to our depths. Moments of connection, moments of beauty all give us a taste of God's presence in our world. The more we are able to recognise them, the more we are able to choose the things which are truly life-giving to us.

Why are you reading this book? Is it because you really feel drawn to reading it? Perhaps a friend recommended it. Or perhaps you bought the book and feel you ought to read it. But perhaps you aren't quite in the mood for it right now. It doesn't really matter; you can wait a bit if this isn't the right time for you.

> *Why are you reading this book?*
> *Is this the right time for you? Are you feeling drawn to it?*
> *Just pay attention and be honest with yourself.*
> *Take some time to talk to God about these things.*

A life of faith

The question at the end of this section asks what it means to live a life of faith. Living a life of faith is more than simply admitting allegiance to a particular belief system. It is more than regular attendance at some form of communal worship. To have any real meaning for you, faith must be a significant factor in your life, rather than just an activity which happens to provide a social circle.

Many people focus on the Hereafter. It is a very Christian idea that professing faith in Jesus is the start of salvation. It is our entry ticket into heaven. I understand where that thinking comes from, and certainly there was a time in my life when my faith was a bit like an insurance policy. At that stage my faith life had a fairly minimal impact on how I lived my 'everyday' life. I wasn't sure whether God existed or not, so I figured that practising my faith was not costing me much, but the alternative could have very serious consequences in the Hereafter. So I judged that on balance I was better off continuing as I was, attending Mass on Sunday and doing a quick five minutes of prayer just before I fell asleep at night.

After making the Spiritual Exercises, my faith shifted from being something important but peripheral in my life, to being central. Relationship with God became my primary concern. Having practised faith in this way, supported by having a daily prayer time for more than a decade, has borne wonderful fruit in my life. I have learnt an enormous amount about myself in the process, and I know that this practice has shaped and changed my interaction with others. It has changed the value system I hold within my life. Not necessarily in terms of what is important to me, but the ordering of the things I count significant. For example, I have come to value my relationships with others far more than my personal achievements. In this way faith is shaping my daily reality. To me, this is the meaning of 'a life of faith' – rather than any particular declaration or assertion of beliefs. The reason I continue to believe is that my belief continues to provide the best framework for my experience, and, through practising my faith, my being has been enriched beyond anything I imagined possible. In this way it has a profound impact on my life on a daily basis. What happens in the Hereafter will take care of itself.

What does faith mean to you, and how does it impact your life? Does it play a central role, or is it something more peripheral?

What does it mean to believe?

What do you believe? It is important here to be honest, regardless of your answer.

Take some time to talk to God about these things.

Noticing where you are – introduction

To know where to place your next step, you need to know where you are right now, and have some idea of your desired destination. The first time I visited London I navigated my way around the city by tube (the network of underground trains). I thoroughly enjoyed the sense of independence and exploration afforded by being able to hop on and off trains and make my way across the city. Then one day someone pointed out to me that some of the stations are much closer together than one might think from looking at the stylised map, so sometimes it's much quicker to take to the streets.

And so I began to explore London on foot. In my twenties I visited both London and Paris frequently and almost always chose to walk rather than use the subway systems, provided the distances weren't too great (and if the weather wasn't bad!).

But before you can plot a route to your destination you have to know where you are. Being dropped somewhere in the middle of central London in the absence of street signs would make navigation to a specific destination virtually impossible. It would be akin to trying to follow the advice a cousin of mine gave to me just a few days after I arrived in Cape Town: 'Just navigate by the mountain.' Knowing the Cape Peninsula as I do now, I realise that the advice made perfect sense, but at the time I didn't know what Table Mountain looked like from different angles, so I didn't know where things were in relation to different aspects of the mountain. It was all a bit of a mystery.

Taking stock then is about taking time to examine where you are in life. So, with each of the exercises, take time to talk to God a little.

The rest of the chapter is probably best read slowly. As I've already said, my suggestion is that you read through each section and then formally pray with the exercise. You could take a morning, or a day, and find a peaceful place which will afford the mental space to engage with the prayer. Or you could read a section a day and take the exercise for that section as your prayer for that day. Of course, you could simply read through the chapter, and come to pray the exercises later, but experience suggests that most people who choose that option don't return to the exercises.

Noticing your surroundings

The question at the end of this section will be about paying attention to your current environment. As you may have gathered, one of the hallmarks of Ignatian spirituality is 'noticing'. Whenever a person starts an individually guided Ignatian retreat, the retreat director will almost always give some advice along the lines of 'pay attention to where you are', or 'take time to mentally arrive here', 'notice the colour of the grass or the leaves on the trees'. This is similar to the idea of mindfulness. It is paying attention to the present. If you are eating, then *eat*: pay attention to flavours and textures of the food. If you are reading then *read*: pay attention to the message, do not try and listen to music at the same time. This noticing of your surroundings is a gentle gathering of what comprises your life at that particular moment.

This can take a number of different forms. The first is the physical spaces that you frequent. Your home and your work space are the spaces which you are most able to craft to your own design. Imagine coming into these spaces – perhaps they are the same place – for the first time. Given the manner in which you appraise space, what would the physical space say to you? Take time to recall, whether people have made any specific comment on entering that space – comments about how they feel about being there, rather than about the physical appearance of the space. For example, I have a few friends who have commented that they love coming over to my flat for supper because it is a safe space for meaningful conversation. This was true even when I had plastic garden furniture in my lounge!

What about the other spaces you frequent – the places you shop, the school your children go to, the church, the library, the park. Why have you chosen those spaces? Do you feel as though you belong when you go there, or do you feel a bit like an interloper who is waiting to be found out? Do you live somewhere that is very different from the place that you grew up in? What factors were involved? The key thing to look out for here is whether you have made a particular choice because it is a good fit for you, or whether you have made the choice because of perceived pressure from someone else. A third option may be that you and the person with whom you have chosen to build your life have had to find a neutral common ground to agree upon. At this stage, do not judge yourself, or your choices, just notice what the driving forces have been. Take time to savour those spaces which feel good – probably chosen because they felt right. Take time to be grateful for those spaces which you have grown into, the spaces which were fairly uncertain to begin with, but have turned out to be a real blessing; the spaces which were foreign but in which you have now made your place.

An important aspect of Ignatian spirituality is growing in understanding of the motivating forces in life. The way in which these forces manifest in different people will vary widely, but they are usually fairly simple at the core. Many of us are strongly motivated by a desire to fit in and be accepted by others, and to be strong and independent. The ways in which we try to achieve this will be different, given variations in circumstance and personality. This exercise of noticing how you have made the choices of the spaces that are in your life is a useful starting point for beginning to understand how these motivating forces operate in your own life.

> *Take some time to call to mind your current environment.*
>
> *Where are you right now? Where do you live? Where do you work?*
>
> *Are these environments working for you at the moment?*
>
> *What factors have influenced the life choices you have made?*
>
> *What are you grateful for?*
>
> *Where are the challenges in your life?*
>
> *Take some time to talk to God about these things.*

Your faith history

Reflecting on your 'faith history' is one of the classic spiritual exercises. It continues to be a useful exercise throughout life because the way we tell our story does change with time. It changes with time precisely because the passage of time brings new perspectives. We get to see how some situations which looked really promising fizzled to nothing, and others which looked hopeless turned out well. We also get to see how things which began as little acorns have grown into something substantial and meaningful: the chance encounter that has blossomed into a valuable companionship; the casual conversation which caused a rethinking of career focus or life priorities. As we go about the intense immediacy of living, it is hard to tell what is going to be truly lasting and what will be a fad. It is also sometimes hard to see where God is in the immediacy of the moment. Some people have a pretty clear answer when asked: 'And where is God in all of that?', but most of us need a bit of time to look at the fruit, before we can attempt an answer to this question.

The faith history exercise at the end of this section offers a way of remembering the highs and lows of one's walk through life – with the express intention of seeking God in the process. In many ways it is a kind of examen[4], but applied to a substantial period of time. It is best to begin the exercise by asking God to show you what God wants you to see. The purpose of the exercise is not to get a stage by stage account of your relationship with God, but rather to allow God to show you where God has been in your life. That is to say, do not worry too much about creating the most accurate account of the development of your faith, rather concentrate on the possibility of encountering God in the process of remembering. This is an important distinction which will return in different guises throughout the book. I am reminded of the Hollywood portrayal of US immigration interviews of married couples to ensure that their relationship is real, not simply one of convenience in order to get a 'Green Card'. Even if answered 'correctly', the questions used there, such as 'Brand of shaving cream?' or 'Type of toothbrush?' do not and cannot prove that a relationship exists. Complete lack of knowledge in this area may be surprising, but there is much more to a real relationship. Similarly, in doing the faith his-

---

4   The examen is sometimes called the review of the day. It is a prayerful reflection on a period of time that has passed. It is discussed in greater detail in Chapter 3.

tory exercise, the emphasis should be on those things which demonstrate real relationship, not simply details of service. You are looking for the moments of joy, gratitude and connection. This is not to say that the more difficult times are to be ignored, they are an important part of the picture too. Hold the moments of encounter before God in gratitude, and then hold the times of difficulty before God. Take time to talk to God a little about what you have found.

The faith history exercise can be applied to one's whole life. It is useful to do it at least once on the whole of your life, and if you have not done it before – or have not done it for many years – now might be a good time. The exercise can also be usefully applied to shorter periods of time. Life is punctuated by several significant transitions – changing jobs, moving, getting married, having children, encountering death, serious illness, divorce, and so on. It might be better to focus only on the period of time since a particular transition has occurred.

Ask God to show you where God has been on your journey through life. Notice the 'mountain tops' and the times of grappling through the 'dense forest'.

Have there been any significant transitions?

Have there been times where major changes have happened in your relationship with God?

Take some time to talk to God about these things.

Who are the people with whom you choose to spend time?

In this process of examining how you are interacting in the world, it is also important to take a step back and consider who you are associating with. Unless you are completely reclusive, your life is likely to be filled with people. Many of them are there by virtue of circumstance – your family of origin and the family you marry into are not chosen. Your colleagues are not chosen if you are working for an organisation. And then there are the people with whom you freely associate. The first part of this new exercise will simply be to look at the different relationships in your life, spend some time identifying those which are life-giving, those which are challenging, and those which seem to be destructive. Notice which people you enjoy spending time with, which people drain you, which people leave you feeling more alive, which people make you think about what you are doing and who you are. One person may fall into many of these categories, and some relationships will change over time. What is true today may not have been the case five years ago, and may not be the case tomorrow.

It is also important to recognise that the way in which we view a relationship is subjective. Any relationship involves two people, and neither holds the full picture of the nature of the relationship. Over time, the behaviour or attitude of the other person will either support our idea of what the relationship is, or not – depending on the extent to which the actual relationship bears out the expectations of both parties.

Some years ago, I gave a workshop at which I suggested that we should try to spend more time with those who bring out the best in us, and gently leave aside those relationships which seem to be destructive. One of the people attending commented that she struggled with one of her colleagues and she was in no position to choose to spend less time with him. This is where it is important to recognise the distinction between those relationships which we choose and those which our life circumstances dictate to us. There are many circumstances under which it is only possible to try to do the best that we can – to examine our own behaviour and try to ensure, in conflictual situations which do not seem to have a solution, that we don't consciously add fuel to the fire. It is also important to be aware that we may have no control over problems we cause for other people.

Almost a decade ago, I was working on a training team. The leader had a logistical role, organising groups, running meetings and so on. Although I had held the position of leader the previous year, the decision had been made not to make me the leader that particular year because I would be playing a key role in the training. A situation of conflict arose between two of the people on the course. Another team member had spoken to me about it, so I took it upon myself to deal with the problem, as I had had direct contact with the people involved on the day that the issue arose. I reported this back to the training team at our daily meeting. About a week or so after the course had ended, I went to talk to our boss to review the course. In the process, I mentioned that I had learnt a few things about myself – that I could, unintentionally, disempower others. At this point my boss looked slightly relieved and said he was glad that I had come to that realisation myself because the team leader had spoken to him about this incident and had been very upset. I was dumbfounded, but went immediately to speak to her and we dealt with the issue. The point is that I didn't know that my behaviour had caused the team leader such angst. I thought I was doing her a favour by smoothing something out before it became a major issue. Whether my action was justified or not, whether it was the best course of action or not, is not the question. I learnt that even simply being myself and getting on and doing things to the best of my ability, with no desire to cause anyone else any problem, can still cause relationships to be damaged. All of us have these kinds of effects on others, whether we are aware of it or not.

This is one of the real complexities of humanity. We *all* carry baggage. People who are able to help us bring our unconscious behaviour into the light will be angels for us. Sometimes this can happen through a loving, nurturing relationship; sometimes it happens through conflict. So conflict can sometimes be useful, but it is a blunt instrument and can simply be destructive. Conflict that does not lead to growing self-awareness should be avoided, or at least minimised, because it will probably serve only to crystallise self-righteousness and stubbornness – and can cause hurt. Not all conflictual relationships can be avoided, but it is worth examining the chosen relationships in your life which do generate conflict: if the conflict is outweighing the loving and nurturing aspects, then there are real questions to be asked about the purpose of the relationship. Would you, as an outsider looking in, regard this particular relationship as a healthy one? If not, then what holds you in that relationship?

Again I take an example from my own experience. When I began my current job, I started getting invitations to join various people for lunch, and for about two years I accepted these invitations. Then one day I realised that the conversation would almost inevitably turn to complaint about some aspect of our working lives. Although I enjoyed the casual contact with people from my university, I just did not like the conversations we were having, and recently I have gently backed away from these invitations. Individually our relationships were good, but as a group we were pulling each other down.

In a different way, there are people that I seek out periodically to have conversation with over a drink or a meal because I value their perspectives and enjoy the conversation. It always takes interesting turns and I come away feeling enriched. I have a few very good friends. It is only in the last year or so that I have truly come to trust them to hold me when I am not okay. In the process of going through a very difficult couple of months, I learnt that there are some people who really will be there for me when I need them. Examining how I am interacting helps me build our mutual trust.

Relationships can constrain one. I have an acquaintance whom I see periodically. She is in her early forties and definitely searching for meaning in life. In many ways she is asking the right questions, but her close friends, for the most part, do not seem to share her search. Most of her close friendships have their origins in high school or university. Whilst they have a great deal of shared history with her, it seems that they are not able to support the part of her which would allow her to shape a very different future.

Ignatian spirituality teaches that it is important, periodically, to pause and ask yourself if the people around you share your values and your passions. If not, then it might be time to bring other voices into your life. It is not necessary to let go of the old friends completely, but you may need to spend less time with them. It is wonderful to have old friends – people who have known you through different phases in your life. The power of shared history should not be underestimated or undervalued, but the pull to maintain the status quo, not to rock the boat, not to change too much, can produce insurmountable inertia to a journey of self-discovery and deepening relationship with God.

There will be spaces – for example your faith community – where your participation is voluntary, but the group is one that is not self-selected. It is open to all. In these kinds of spaces, it is common to find people who may seem to share the same ideals, but who are not a natural fit for you. In these sorts of spaces withdrawal is not a good option. The invitation is to find a way to co-exist for the benefit of the bigger picture. I find aspects of my parish community most challenging in this respect, but, at the same time I have become, through this interaction, far more aware of the diversity of gifts that people have, and it has helped me realise that any community needs this diversity in order to thrive.

Who are the important people in your life at the moment?

Who are the people who are angels to you – the people who bring light, joy and peace into your life?

Who are the people to whom you are an angel?

Who are the people who challenge you, who reveal sides of yourself you would rather not see?

Take some time to talk to God about these things.

Goals, desires and dreams

Our goals, desires and dreams change over time. Think back to high school: what were your goals and dreams then? Where did you want to be? What career did you envision? Did you imagine marriage and children? How much of what you thought then is a part of your reality now? Before we go any further, I must admit that I had no long term goals at that stage, I was not sure what career I would have and I had no real desire to marry or have children. So do not worry too much if you cannot remember, or did not have a clear picture. Maybe the question to consider is what your high school self might think about your life now. I am deeply grateful to be able to say that my life is far richer than I would have imagined it could be. I love my job, I have some fantastic friends, I spend time hiking and walking, I am able to work part-time as a spiritual director. I have good family relationships and I have been blessed with some excellent mentors along the way. Perhaps most importantly, I have discovered that relationships are crucial to my well-being, and I have people who are willing to be my friends.

Looking back at who you were then and who you are now is an important part of taking stock. It may be that high school is too far removed from your current reality to be able to use it as the point of contrast in this exercise. Perhaps think about the time before you had children, or the time before your children left home. Maybe think about working in a previous career, or a time before a significant relationship began, or ended. Nevertheless, if high school is not too far removed it is probably one of the most useful comparisons, because it is the version of yourself before the reality of having to take care of yourself started to shape your dreams.

One of the strangest phenomena in our world today (particularly for the middle class) is the creation of a life which then serves as a trap. As we earn more, so we gradually increase our expectations. We buy more expensive cars and bigger houses. We eat out more often and refine our palates with respect to wines. Our holidays become more exotic. Very quickly, the idea of returning to the simple life we had when we began working becomes increasingly unappealing. We are trapped by the very life we have created, because it seems impossible to downsize.

It is crucial that we are able to look at our lives with a bit of wisdom. It is not that having stuff is inherently evil. No, returning to the Principle and Foundation of *The Spiritual Exercises*, we are to use the things in this world to help us towards our end (deeper relationship with God, with others, with ourselves and with creation) and to set things aside when they interfere with that end. So the question is always: Where is this taking me? For example, when you have a family, priorities such as education and providing good opportunities for your children are important considerations. But if you are crippling yourself financially to send your children to private schools to keep up with the neighbours, or to be socially acceptable in a particular circle, you may want to re-think the importance of this.

Our goals, dreams and desires are likely to change and grow and develop as we engage with life and begin to get to know ourselves better. The ideals we might have had in order to keep our parents happy, or to live up to certain expectations, may well change. Different priorities come into play at different stages of life. The problem arises when those shifts happen unconsciously. This could be the classic mid-life crisis. Suddenly you realise that you have created a life that you never intended to live. The dreams and desires you had in your youth seem to be a faint memory and there is an urgency to reclaim them before it is too late. It is therefore important to look periodically at your goals, dreams and desires. To notice what is shifting and what remains the same – precisely so that you will not wake up with a shock one day to discover just how far you have strayed from what you intended. This is true, no matter what your age[5].

---

5   My editor says so – she's 70.

What were your goals, dreams and desires when you were younger?
Where are you now? How do you feel about that?
What are you goals, dreams and desires now?
Take some time to talk to God about these things.

Use of time

The way we use our time is directly linked to our goals, dreams and desires. If you are not dedicating any of your time to achieving those things which you say you want, then they are not going to happen. So how do you use your time? This is not a question you can answer simply, or easily. Obviously it is important to pay attention to the things that are life-giving to us, and to choose them consciously. However, not everything that is worthwhile is enjoyable. So we need to be careful not to dismiss things too quickly just because they don't feel as if they are fulfilling. This is the trap of the instant gratification society.

It is important to notice the things which are life-giving for you at the moment. What activities leave you feeling invigorated, or contented, or appreciative of life? Is the way in which you spend your leisure time enjoyable? Do you feel that your job is worthwhile? Do you enjoy what you do?

But be aware – an oversimplified dualism can emerge: productive activity good; leisure activity bad. Not so; not everything we do needs to have a 'higher purpose' to be a 'good' use of time. We don't need to spend every instant doing things that are obviously productive. There are some activities – like spending time with infant children – which can be incredibly boring, but are a very important investment in the future, and clearly the 'right thing to do'. Cooking good, nutritious meals or taking regular exercise can also fall into this category. These things may not seem significant or stimulating at the time, but they are a vital investment in your health. Sometimes even an afternoon nap, or vegging in front of the television can be a good way to get some time-out. A healthy balance needs to be struck between productive time and 'vegetation' time. Where the balance lies will depend on the level of mental and emotional stress in your life and on what you use as your primary escape mechanism. If you escape into activity, then you may find that in times of stress you go into overdrive. If you escape into avoidance, then during times of stress, levering yourself off the couch may be very difficult. One is not better or worse than the other; it is simply important to *be aware what your drivers are*; this will make you more likely to hear the warning bell, and recognise when you are out of balance – so that you can take steps to deal with the stressors, as far as you are able to.

In addition, there may be a good reason for putting the active pursuit of a particular goal on hold. This might be when you have young children, or perhaps when someone close to you has a life-threatening illness, or for some other significant reason. This is not necessarily a problem, it should just be consciously noted, and your choice should be reassessed periodically, even if the external circumstances do not change. It's important that you be aware that the choice to put this goal on hold was, and is, yours to make. Do not make someone's illness or death, or the needs of your child, the main reason for not pursuing this goal. That is an unfair burden to place on the other. The uncomfortable truth may be that you are afraid of failing if you do pursue your goal and the situation gives you the perfect excuse not to try.

Nonetheless, even if you are in a state of reasonable equilibrium, it is important to look at the way in which you allocate your time to different tasks. I have been wanting to write this book for several years, but it is only recently that I decided to allocate a substantial chunk of time to actually writing it. I had about a third of the book already written, and I needed to take time to figure out what I needed to add to that, and to give time to editing it. After a period of about six months I finally got around to it. And yes, I had been busy with all sorts of things, and there are good reasons why writing the book at an earlier time was problematic. But two things held me back: fear of failure, and the fact that I did not actively allocate time to the task.

Another useful illustration is my passion for hiking. Walking in nature is a deeply restorative activity for me. When I lived in the UK I bought a lot of kit; I bought maps; I bought books of walks in different areas; but I only actually went hiking on a few occasions. I think that this kind of pseudo-activity or imagined activity happens a great deal, aided by the internet and access to all sorts of information and pictures of the things that we say we like to do. If my interest in hiking were judged solely by the amount of time I actually spent walking at that time, it would have been considered a minor hobby. Most of us indulge in similar pseudo-activities.

> *How are you using your time?*
>
> *What aspects of your daily life do you savour and enjoy, relishing the time you spend on them?*
>
> *What aspects of your daily life do you find difficult, resenting the time they take?*
>
> *How do you spend your leisure time? How do you feel about this?*
>
> *Take some time to talk to God about these things.*

Drawing the pieces together

Do not judge yourself at this stage; what you are doing here is simply putting the pieces out on the table in front of you and examining what is there. Do not rush on to the next chapter until you have a fairly good sense of where you are at the moment and of how you feel about that.

> *Ask yourself again: What are the important things in my internal landscape at the moment?*
>
> *What are the pressures?*
>
> *Where are the invitations?*

33

Chapter 2: Who is God?

God created man in His image and then man
returned the favour
— George Bernard Shaw

K nowing ourselves to the best of our ability is an important part of the spiritual journey. However, it is equally
important to look at the God to whom we are trying to relate.
This chapter is about exploring our images of God – because
these images profoundly influence our faith journey.

••

Pause for a moment and notice the God who is with you.

Who is that God?

What is that God like?

It is important to tease out the difference between what we
say we believe and how we actually operate. We do not have
to aim immediately for congruency between these two, but
an awareness of a gap between what we say we believe and
how we operate gives us a starting point to deepening our
faith journey.

It is important to realise that we all experience this gap; for
some it is bigger than for others. Do not be disappointed in
yourself if you start noticing such a gap within yourself. As
we begin this exploration, simply hold before God in prayer
the desire to know God better. Part of that increase in knowledge will be a growing awareness of the discrepancies buried
deep within.

Images of God

One of the most common stumbling blocks to a healthy and vibrant prayer life is our image of God. It is one of the things we hardly ever take time to examine or question. This is particularly true for those of us who have been brought up in a specific religious tradition. If this has been compounded by teachers or parents using the idea that 'God is always watching you' as a tool to ensure good behaviour, we can end up with a very warped image of God. Even if it did not happen in quite this way, our image of God is one area of our faith lives which frequently goes unquestioned or unexamined. We presume, because we have heard the message that God is a loving God, that this is in fact the God to whom we are trying to relate. The result is a disjuncture between the God we say we believe in, and the God we actually believe in. So interrogating our own image of God can feel as though we're interrogating the reality of God. Many of us simply do not go there and, as a result, many of us persist in carrying around images of God which are just not helpful.

Uncovering those images is an important part of growing in our faith. A rich and fruitful life of faith can begin to take root only when we start to discover that God does truly care; that God does truly want the best for us; and, most importantly, that God's love is truly unconditional. In his book *The God of Surprises*, Gerard W Hughes, SJ[6], gives a graphic caricature – he even calls God 'Good old Uncle George' – describing the kind of spiritual schizophrenia we can find ourselves suffering from. Hughes's basic premise is that we somehow manage not to notice the hideous image of God we are carrying – an image which insists that we proclaim that 'God is a loving God', whilst at the same time fearing that God will smite us if we do something even just a little bit wrong:

> God was a family relative, much admired by Mum and
> Dad, who described him as very loving, a great friend

---

6   SJ: A member of the Society of Jesus, usually referred to as a Jesuit.

of the family, very powerful and interested in all of us. Eventually we are taken to visit 'Good Old Uncle George'. He lives in a formidable mansion, is bearded, gruff and threatening. We cannot share our parents' professed admiration for this jewel in the family. At the end of the visit, Uncle George turns to address us. 'Now listen, dear,' he begins, looking very severe, 'I want to see you here once a week, and if you fail to come, let me show you what will happen to you.' He then leads us down to the mansion's basement. It is dark, becomes hotter and hotter as we descend, and we begin to hear unearthly screams. In the basement there are steel doors. Uncle George opens one. 'Now look in there, dear', he says. We see a nightmare vision, an array of blazing furnaces with little demons in attendance, who hurl into the blaze those men, women and children who fail to visit Uncle George or to act in a way he approved. 'And if you don't visit me, dear, that is where you will most certainly go', says Uncle George. He then takes us upstairs again to meet Mum and Dad. As we go home, tightly clutching Dad with one hand and Mum with the other, Mum leans over us and says, 'And now don't you love Uncle George with all you heart and soul, mind and strength?' And we, loathing the monster, say 'Yes I do,' because to say anything else would be to join the queue at the furnace. At a tender age religious schizophrenia has set in and we keep telling Uncle George how much we love him, how good he is and that we want to do only what pleases him. We observe what we are told are his wishes and dare not admit, even to ourselves, that we loathe him[7].'

Obviously the image is a caricature. Nevertheless, many of us carry vestiges of this kind of image into adult life. On a fairly rudimentary level, if we have ever been subject to an

---

7   Gerard W. Hughes (1996) p.34.

authority figure who used the idea that 'God sees everything we do' to shame us into good behaviour, then we are primed for the Uncle George experience. Even if we manage to shake off those immature experiences, we still find strong voices of disapproval in our church communities: voices which will tell us unequivocally that we cannot possibly call ourselves Christian if we do such and such, or think such and such. So we have the experience within our faith communities of having to live up to a certain standard – or face eviction. If we never really grapple with our faith and our understanding of God, we are left with this terrible image which we do not dare to look at for fear of questioning what it might mean. But it requires a little risk taking, a smidgeon of soul searching, some serious questioning topped with paying attention to our actual experience of God to begin to discover that God is indeed loving.

We find it difficult to believe in unconditional love. We may believe that unconditional love is theoretically possible, but we also somehow believe that God's unconditional love is only for some mythical perfect version of ourselves which we continue to fall short of. The truth is that we find it hard to love ourselves, and to accept ourselves, with all our shortcomings. We presume that, because we find ourselves to be less than lovable, God sees us that way too. This idea is reinforced by judgmental faith communities. As many people have said: 'God made us in God's image and we have been returning the favour ever since'. This is absolutely true, we do create God in our own image, but this human-patterned version of God is a gross distortion of the reality. If unconditional love does exist, it must *be unconditional*. God must love us regardless of what we do. God must love us as we are today, with all the complexity and imperfection and failure that we carry. God must love us, even when we are disappointed in ourselves, even when we find it almost impossible to face ourselves, let alone love ourselves. This is not to suggest that God may not be disappointed by some of the things we choose, or that God may not experience profound sadness at some of ways we treat each other. But God loves us nonetheless. The gospels are filled with examples of Jesus acting in precisely this way – choosing to engage in a caring and loving manner with those who, through their actions or lifestyle, had been found wanting by the faith community.

It is probably worthwhile pointing out here that Ignatian spirituality is what is called a 'cataphatic' spirituality. This is a spirituality which makes use of our human understanding of love, relationships and personhood to give us a starting point in understanding God. This is, of its nature, limited and erroneous, but we have to begin somewhere; we can describe God only in terms of the qualities we know. The model that we have in the person of Jesus gives us good reason to trust that we can indeed start here, recognising that God is beyond this limited beginning.

Facing ourselves

One of the dynamics of a healthy prayer life is the emergence of a recognition of the significance of sin. But this dynamic will not emerge until we have a healthy, robust sense of the love of God. Ignatius recognised this movement, and so the build-up to making the Spiritual Exercises is immersion of ourselves in God's love for us. Crucially, it is followed, in the First Week, by exercises designed to put us in touch with sin.

The grace of the First Week of the Spiritual Exercises is the grace of the loved sinner. The experience is quite profound. Once I feel myself firmly rooted in a sense of God's love for the world and a sense of God's love for me, I examine myself and my life, and see that there are many areas in which I fail myself and in which I hurt those around me. Some of those areas exist because of what has happened to me. Some are personality-driven, and, crushingly, some are simply what I have chosen. In this experience I discover that *God truly loves me as I am*. I no longer need to hide parts of myself from God, because in this series of exercises I have sat, in the presence of God, with the parts of myself which I do not particularly enjoy. The experience of the sense of God's love remains tangible and does not fade as I dare to expose my sins to God. Of course God knows my sin, but choosing to consciously reveal my sin to God, through consciously revealing it to myself, is a powerful change in the dynamic of my relationship with God. I can begin to trust that I do not need to hide any facet of myself from God.

Some traditions have developed rituals around ways to deal with sin. In both the Roman Catholic and high Anglican traditions there is a formal, sacramental process of reconciliation. This usually takes place in the form of a conversation between a priest and the person confessing. It has a specific form which includes a confession by the person of the things for which they seek God's forgiveness, and a formal absolution by the priest. There is usually some form of penance given by the priest, most frequently in the form of prayer. In some ways, the sacrament of reconciliation, as powerful and wonderful as it is, can sometimes serve to underline the false image we have that God can love us only if we are good. The main purpose of the sacrament of reconciliation is not to repair God's love for us. It is for us to clear the debris so that we can dare to make conversation with God again.

In all of the Church's traditions, we can get caught up in the significance of ritual or other 'indicators'. With those traditions which are strongly oriented towards sacramental worship, we sometimes need to be reminded that God does not need us to participate in the sacraments as some kind of 'qualifying criterion' before God will communicate with us. No, we need the sacraments *because they help us*. They remind us of who God is, and that God loves us and wants the best for us. They help us get past our own debris. If love is not accessible to every single person in every single state of being, it is not unconditional love, and not one of us can trust it.

Really looking at oneself with honesty is never easy. It requires that we both take credit for the good and responsibility for the not so good. All of us are mixed bag of giftedness and brokenness. The way in which we interact in any given situation is normally some kind of mixture of the two. And if we try to do it alone and fail in some way, we often get caught up in a sense of guilt or regret. Our failures leap out at us and we find it hard to recognise our real giftedness. Sometimes we get caught in a web of bitterness – remembering times when people have wronged us. When we begin such an exploration of sin, it is absolutely crucial that we are rooted in a solid experience of God's love.

Returning to the idea of the image of God: it is important for me first to look at who I understand God to be; to spend time noticing my own image of God, because there is often a mismatch between what I say I believe about God – my espoused or theoretical image – and the real or operational image which affects how I actually behave and relate to God. Most of us have, to a greater or lesser extent, unhealthy images of God left over from childhood. Images we have perhaps never really challenged, or have simply accepted. In the Christian tradition, we have the founding story of a God who was willing to go to the most extreme lengths to help us to understand God's love for us. God literally accepted death to get us to wake up and see that God loves us.

In all of our Christian traditions we have developed strange and warped understandings which undermine our belief in the unconditional love of God. Practices around the Eucharist can be most revealing in this respect. In some of the strong reformed traditions, partaking in communion is not a frequent occurrence. This is partly out of a distorted sense of the respect. After all, scripture tells us we should not partake of communion if we are not in good faith with one another. So it is considered better to minimise the possibility of receiving communion when we are not in good standing by minimising the opportunity to partake in communion. It also means that we have plenty of time between receiving communion to get ourselves in 'right standing' with God. However, this entirely fails to take into consideration the point that it is precisely by partaking in communion that we are transformed. We are never worthy, but God is always generous. There is something profoundly powerful about sharing communion with one another.

There are many scripture readings which talk of God's passion for us:

Psalm 23 — The Lord is my shepherd, I shall not want. He makes me lie down in green pastures; he leads me beside still waters; he restores my soul.

John 3:16 — For God so loved the world he gave his only Son, so that everyone who believes in him may not perish but may have eternal life.

Psalm 139: 1-5 — Oh Lord, you have searched me and known me. You know when I sit down and when I rise up; you discern my thoughts from far away. You search out my path and my lying down, and are acquainted with all my ways. Even before a word is on my tongue, O Lord, you know it completely. You hem me in, behind and before, and lay your hand upon me.

Isaiah 43: 1-2 — But now thus says the Lord, he who created you, O Jacob, he who formed you, O Israel: Do not fear I have redeemed you; I have call you by your name, you are mine. When you pass through the waters, I will be with you, and through the rivers, they shall not overwhelm you, when you walk through fire you shall not be burned, and the flame shall not consume you.

We have, too, the wonderful series of parables in Luke 15. God does not forget us, even if we stray.

Unfortunately, even the most inspirational of biblical passages is insufficient for most of us. Simply reading the passage confirms our theoretical understanding of who God is, but unless we stop and notice what we actually feel about God and about the passage, we fail to notice the internal disparity. We fear God, and not in a good way. We are told that it is good to have God in our lives, but so many of us are terrified of what that might actually mean. Mostly, we fear that we might have to give something up. For many young people there is a fear that we might be called to the priesthood or religious life, or to become a missionary. For older people there may be a fear that we might have to take something on or give something up. Sometimes we simply have a general fear that who we are is not good enough or is somehow flawed.

Your own experience – who is the God who is with you?

Let us start, this time, with an exercise.

Pause for a moment and remember a time when you felt particularly close to God. It does not matter what the occasion was, it does not matter when it was. Maybe it happened yesterday; maybe it was some years ago. It does not matter. Just take a moment to really remember – where were you, who were you with, what was going on, was there anything particularly significant happening in your life at that stage? Notice the feeling that you had at that time.

When asked this kind of question, most people associate feelings of joy, peace, contentment, being loved, being accepted with such moments of encounter. In these moments, if we can just give God space to be God, we discover a God who is compassionate, kind and caring; a God who is truly for us. The problem, for so many of us though, is that we find it so hard to allow God to be God. If we are trying to pray in such moments, we may immediately begin by telling God why we cannot possibly do what we assume God is going to ask of us. Or we begin to chastise ourselves for some minor sin. We do not actually give God a chance to speak.

Another reason that we avoid God can be that we do not want to face ourselves. We are afraid that if we stand before God we will be stripped of our ego defences. That can feel quite scary. Whilst it is true that in time we do come to face ourselves when we deepen relationship with God, we forget the most important quality of God: Not only is God loving, compassionate, forgiving, slow to anger and rich in kindness – God is incredibly gentle.

God is also extremely patient. God does not push faster than we are comfortable moving. When you really allow yourself to dare to trust those moments of encounter with God, slowly something in you begins to open in that space. I was talking to a group of young people about prayer a while ago. One of them asked: 'Why do we pray if God knows everything about us?' We pray because God is not invasive. God waits for us to reveal ourselves to God. In the act of prayer, we begin to speak to God about the things that are truly important to us. Most of us begin on safe ground, talking to God about the straightforward stuff in our lives, and slowly, as we persist in prayer, we begin talking about the more important things, the dreams we have, the woundings, the times we have failed. It is only when we consciously begin to talk to God about the less easy stuff that we discover what it really means in our lives.

In the latter part of 2010, I went through a most powerful period of healing. A major wounding happened in my life a long time ago. And over the years I have periodically tracked over the ground in prayer, each time understanding a little more the depth of the wounding. In November 2009 a particular event triggered my memory of that wounding. As I sat with it in prayer, and explored it with my spiritual director, I realised that that wounding had had an influence on how I made decisions and how I lived my life. I also saw how I had inadvertently caused others pain by operating out of my wounded space. Over the months, I was slowly able to allow God into that space, and to allow God to love me in my brokenness. As I have already mentioned in this chapter, the grace of the First Week of Spiritual Exercises is to know myself to be a loved sinner, that is to say, a moment of clarity when I have seen my sin and my brokenness – and I have felt totally loved by God. I have encountered that grace several times in my life. It is utterly disarming. In those moments I understand the power of redemption. God does not need me to be good or to be perfect, God just needs me to allow God to love me. In those moments, and in the aftermath, I find that I am far more grateful and far more generous. I am far more able to forgive the failings of those around me, and I am far more compassionate to those who are broken.

God does not need anything from you. God simply loves you, because God is love and God finds you to be loveable. Not because you are good. Not because you go to church five times a week. Not because you help in the soup kitchen. God loves you because you are you. There is no 'and', and no 'but' in that sentence. God loves you. And you know that to be true. Not because you have been told so, or because you have read it in the Bible. You know it to be true because at some point in your life you have had a glimpse of that already.

In her poem 'The Ponds[8]', Mary Oliver describes the beauty of a carpet of lilies on a pond: 'I bend closer and see | how this one is clearly lopsided— | and this one wears an orange blight— | and this one a glossy cheek | half nibbled away— | and that one is a slumped purse | full of its own | unstoppable decay'. The point is simply that the whole can be beautiful even when the fine detail is flawed.

Conclusion

At the heart of Ignatian spirituality then, is an expectation that sooner or later God will show up. In his autobiography,

---

8   Mary Oliver (2012) p.58.

Ignatius writes that even if the Bible were to be taken from him, he would still believe in the power of the love of God. He believed because he had experienced it, not because a detailed analysis of the Bible convinced him that it was true. Faith, if it is to have any impact on our lives, cannot just be intellectual; it must be visceral. Making the Spiritual Exercises provides a space in which encounter with God can happen, but it is just one such space. Even so, there are many who have pored over the text and failed to engage with the experience it provides. In all our faith traditions it is possible for us to cling to the words, but fail to hear the message. To concentrate only on the words is to miss the essence. It is to stand staring at the finger and miss the moon it is pointing towards.

Who is the God that you relate to?

Who is the God that keeps you faithful to your spiritual practice?

When in your life have you caught a glimpse of the God who truly loves you?

Take some time to talk to God about these things.

Chapter 3: Finding God in all Things

Pray as you can, not as you can't. Take yourself as you find yourself and start from that
— *Dom John Chapman*

God can be found present and active in the minutiae of life. If you want to live a life in which you are more conscious of God's presence, then a good place to start is the development of practices and rituals which help you to pay attention to God. The more you practice noticing God, the more likely you are to spot God in the midst of the craziness, or the humdrum, of life. Prayer is the name we give to the practice of noticing God. So before we launch into a discussion on prayer and different ways of praying, think about the questions: What helps me pay attention to God? What makes me feel distant from God? What is prayer for me? Why do I pray?

Do not worry about what 'counts' as prayer; simply take a few moments to remember some of the occasions of connection with God you have experienced over the last while.

Why do we pray?

I remember asking myself this question when I was in my final year at university: Why do I pray? I was lying on my bed shortly before switching out my light and I was reading one of those small booklets which had a short scripture passage for each day, a short paragraph relating the scripture passage to life and a couple of questions. As I lay in bed that particular night, I remember wondering what I was doing, because it seemed pretty pointless. I would spend about five minutes each night going through the same process, and it seemed to me that it was making absolutely no difference to anything.

I think at that stage in my life I was still very much operating under the assumption that God had a balance sheet (much like what we were examining in the previous chapter), and that prayer counted in the 'good stuff' column. And you had to make sure that the 'good stuff' column outweighed the 'bad stuff' column. I remember quite clearly thinking: If God does exist, and I spend five minutes in prayer a night – it doesn't cost a whole lot and I'll be okay at the end of the day. And if God does not exist then, it doesn't cost a whole lot and it can't hurt. I call this type of prayer 'prayer as insurance policy'.

That kind of prayer is, tragically, the kind of prayer that so many of us end up using for far longer than we should. It is the kind of prayer that happens when we have outgrown some of our ideas of God, but have not yet had the courage to grapple with our image of God.

So it is important to ask the question –

Why do you pray?

The real reason that we pray is important. It is important because examining that alone can lead us into deeper relationship with God. For me, noticing my 'insurance policy' prayer influenced my decision to go on an Alpha course, which opened the door to trying a six week retreat in daily life[9], which in turn opened the door to Ignatian spirituality for me.

---

9   The Ignatian phrase 'a retreat in daily life' refers to a period time – short or long – during which one sees a spiritual director about once week, and commits to praying each day, for perhaps half an hour, over that period.

That kind of story is not unique to me. Some years ago I was accompanying a middle-aged woman on a week of guided prayer. I forget her exact words, but I remember in our first conversation her saying something to effect that if she did not find God that week, she would leave the Church. She was going to show up and participate fully in the spiritual direction and make time for the prayer, but this was God's last chance. Not only did she find God that week, but I have stayed in touch with her over the years, and, having made a number of retreats, she made the Spiritual Exercises a few years ago, and has recently been trained as a spiritual director herself. All of that was made possible, because she was brutally honest with herself and with me. She dared to admit that she was not really convinced by the whole 'God story'. In confronting herself and her beliefs she gave God the fraction of an inch God needs to be able to reveal Godself to us. God does not need us to be good, but God does need honesty.

So we return to that powerful question – why do you pray?

I think one of my all-time favourite responses to that question comes from the film *Shadowlands*. In the film, CS Lewis is trying to make sense of his wife's illness. A friend comments that he (Lewis) has been so faithful to his prayer that God must surely respond. To which Lewis replies: 'I don't pray because it changes God; I pray because it changes me.'

This leads us into the second big question –

How does prayer 'work'?

The truth is, we simply do not know how prayer works. We know that God loves us, and we know instinctively that prayer is a good thing. But we really do not know how it works. Sometimes people have 'miraculous healings', sometimes they do not. Why is that? Some people seem to have such tough lives, while others seem to sail through. Why is that? Honestly, we do not know. And seeking answers to those kinds of questions leads us up a blind alley where we are left with the most appalling choice – either God is a monster, or God simply does not care about this particular circumstance. Either way, the god we find down that alley is not God at all. *Cannot* be God at all.

Many people have tried to offer analogies to explain the strange complexity of life. Perhaps one of the best is that the life we see is a bit like the reverse of a tapestry, an unfathomable chaos of coloured threads, but, as with any analogy, if we push too far we end up in trouble. I am not going to propose any alternative, I am simply going to offer you words I wrote some time ago: 'I recognise now that I don't understand how prayer works, but I know it is slowly transforming me – and that is enough.'

In the Gospel of Matthew it is written: 'By their fruit you shall know them' (Matt 7:16 and 7:20). In the context Matthew is referring to false prophets, but I think that idea can be extended a little. Prayer practices can be judged by the fruit shown in the life of the person who is praying. In my own experience, the fruit of prayer is utterly extraordinary. I can say without any doubt whatsoever, that I am the person that I am today, because I am a person of prayer. Sitting in prayer with my uncertainty, with my lack of faith, with my brokenness has led me to believe in the power of redemption. If this truly is the fruit of prayer, I will lend my voice to those who cry out about the importance of prayer in our lives.

Through prayer I have learnt about love, forgiveness, healing. I have learnt to sit with my pain, my anger, my disappointment. I have learnt to sit with it until it begins to shift – slowly, slowly it begins to take a new shape. The experience is not forgotten, but the feeling has shifted; something new is emerging. Sometimes it is insight; sometimes compassion; sometimes forgiveness; and eventually (although this can take a good while) joy. I have witnessed that process within myself over and over and over again. I am beginning to trust that dynamic – precisely because I know that I am transformed in the process. And I know that life is long and complex, and I will need this grace again.

In his book, *Breathing, I Pray*, my friend and former colleague Ivan Mann puts it this way:

> When life has been traumatic for us it is too easy to listen only to the crashing sounds – the pains that have been inflicted on us and which we have inflicted on others, the misunderstandings and betrayals that make our relationships go awry. We can listen to these for eternity and allow them to continue to build up our resentments or sense of victimisation ... OR ... we can listen beneath those loud aggressive sounds to the deeper sound of God trying to be heard above the din. If we do that there will be a dying in us of things we need to release and in the dying a reception of new life. This dying will not deny those darker things but will transform their energy into that which is life-giving. Somehow this deeper listening can allow us both to re-lease and receive – not to release the past or its impact on us, but to release us from bondage to it, release us for what is to come[10].

Pause before you continue, and notice the places in your life where you see the fruit of prayer.

What then is prayer?

Here I think it is helpful if we make a distinction between formal prayer and the ongoing experience of living in the presence of God. I will say something about formal prayer in a little while, but before I get there, I want to return to the

---

10   Ivan Mann (2005) p.3.

heart of this book – the spirituality of Ignatius of Loyola. Ignatius was a man of profound prayer – some of his experiences make it clear that he was a mystic. But he was also a man of action. There are some phrases commonly associated with Ignatian spirituality – one of them is 'finding God in all things'. As I sit writing these words I am watching the sun setting behind Table Mountain. The mountain is a silhouette, the sky still light, and clouds a vibrant pink. The invitation for me is simply to watch. To be present to this moment. To be grateful for this moment. To notice God in this moment. This is prayer.

In her poem, 'The Summer Day[11]', Mary Oliver describes the movement of a grasshopper and then makes the observation that she doesn't know what prayer is, but she does know how to pay attention: 'how to kneel in the grass, how to be idle and blessed, how to stroll through the fields...'.

The beginning and the end of prayer is: Being Present. We cannot possibly notice God's presence unless we are able to be present to the solid, tangible world around us. It begins with this. And ultimately, for the vast majority of us, prayer will lead us back into an awareness of the world around us. To begin, we need to notice where we are – and how we are – right now.

Take a moment to notice how you are right now – in this moment.

Where are you? What can you see? What can you hear?

Is it warm or cold? Peaceful or chaotic?

Are you focusing on these words, or is your mind preoccupied? Maybe you are distracted by the people around you. Maybe you are waiting for a phone call, or a message. Perhaps you are just distracted by wondering what to cook tonight...

If you can, just stop a moment, and notice yourself in your world right now. Be present.

---

11   Mary Oliver (2012) p.60.

There is an old story which is told in many different ways. The way I remember it is this: An old peasant man frequently visits a church. He takes a seat in one of the pews and sits quietly for a long period. One day the priest approaches him and asks him what he is doing when he sits there. The man responds simply: 'I look at God and God looks at me.'

While most of us desire that sense of connection, it does not usually come immediately. For many of us, that sense of communion and communication is at least a few steps away from where we are now. But it is important to recognise that we cannot just will ourselves into a place of connection. The only entry point is where we are right now. Once again, the invitation is to honesty. Do not try to pretend that you are anywhere other than exactly where you are. God is not fooled – and no one else cares. When you pause to try to pray, if you are stressed and distracted: Start There. Tell God that you are stressed and distracted. Tell God that you are frustrated that you cannot seem to leave these distractions behind. Or tell God what is on your mind. Nothing disrupts a healthy prayer life as much as trying to fool God – or fool yourself? – into thinking that you are just fine when you are not.

If we can dare to live out of the belief that God is still patiently labouring in us – that God is not finished with us yet, then maybe we can let go of some of our hang-ups about prayer. Once, when I was a student, I was on a weekend retreat led by Thomas Plastow SJ, the assistant chaplain of the university. During one of the prayer periods, Thomas led us through a prayer exercise – an exercise of the imagination – in which you imagine that you are a statue and then Jesus comes to view the statue, and you see Jesus' reaction to you. The exercise ends with a conversation with Jesus. On this occasion I saw the statue of myself as a work in progress. The statue was clearly not yet complete, but Jesus was still delighted to see how the work was progressing. I remember this occasion in particular because I realised that I did not have to have my life perfected before I could start making a contribution. This experience freed me to continue to grow; to do what I could, accepting who I was at that time. I did not need to wait until I had it all sorted; I could trust that, in engaging with life, the statue would slowly be completed. God did not require me to be 'complete' (whatever that could possibly mean) before God could use me.

> Much of our ability to take risks with prayer depends on believing that God is still labouring for us, and that he gives us life as a gift to be enjoyed. It depends on believing that God will not reject us if we are not always earnest but sometimes just rejoice in his gifts. It's the difference between a child who has been taught dutifully to say 'Thank you' for a present and the one who may be just as dutiful but who shows their gratitude in deeds by enjoying the gift they have been given[12].

If we can trust that where we are now, this very day, is exactly where we are supposed to be, we have a place to start. If we can let God be God, and trust that God can carry us just as far as God needs us to go, we can let go of the paralysing feeling that we ought somehow to be further along than we are. If we give in to that feeling we will stop making any progress because we have sacrificed the most important thing we need to take a step forward in faith – honesty: honesty with ourselves, and honesty with God.

Whilst this practice of active attention or noticing is fundamental to prayer, there is something more that happens when we take time to be still. My brother-in-law Phil Starks writes of an experience of walking on his own in the woods near his house:

> It's darker now, under these trees, and my thoughts turn more inward. I enjoy the process of individual

---

12   Ivan Mann (2005) p.6.

thoughts transitioning into an internal conversation, and I have long stopped fearing those rare occasions when the conversation becomes unpredictable, unfamiliar[13].

To me, this is prayer. The combination of being alone and quiet; simply thinking about things in the presence of God, and then finding myself surprised by the interior conversation, is something I seek when I pray. But that experience very rarely happens to me unless I am alone and either intentionally praying, or walking. It can happen in other situations, but only very occasionally. Nevertheless, the point is that taking time out for formal prayer provides the mental space required for this kind of connection to occur. God can communicate without a formal prayer time, but the formal prayer time increases our receptivity for that communication.

There are probably as many ways of praying as there are people in the world. No one form of prayer is better or worse than another, but some forms of prayer will work better for you at whatever stage you are at now. Again, going back to the Principle and Foundation, use those things which help you towards your goal, and gently set aside those things which do not. As Dom John Chapman once wrote: 'Pray as you can, not as you can't. Take yourself as you find yourself and start from that.' (So do not get caught up on the technique and detail expressed in the rest of this chapter. I have offered a variety because it is helpful to know at least some simple ways of praying.)

The Examen

Finding God in the midst of our daily lives can be challenging. One of the most useful prayers to this end is a short re-

---

13   Philip T Starks (2012)

flection on the highs and lows of the day. It is a simple but powerful act of paying attention to God's presence in our lives. The formal way in which this is handed down in the Ignatian tradition is through the practice of the examen. It is often said that Ignatius would allow the Jesuits to leave aside all other forms of prayer in pursuit of their ministry, but under no circumstances were they allowed to abandon the examen. It is a prayer which actively encourages us to pay attention to God's presence in our daily reality. As we do this we will almost certainly become aware of areas where we have stumbled. We notice and note them. And go on.

Sadly, some time between Ignatius' writing of *The Spiritual Exercises* in the mid-1500s, and the 1950s, the purpose of the examen got somewhat warped. Many of the older generation of Roman Catholics may have a rather negative recollection of the way they were taught to 'examine their conscience'. It is therefore worthwhile looking at the difference between an examination of conscience and an examination of consciousness. The examination of conscience is probably best explained by a caricature; it was used to develop a 'laundry list' of one's sins. Penitents were encouraged to repent of these sins and ask forgiveness for them, and were probably expected to perform some act of penance. I have no doubt that some people benefited from this process, but for others an unhealthy over-scrupulousness flourished with this practice. Of course it is worthwhile to come to a greater knowledge and understanding of one's personal faults and failings, and I would certainly contend that it is only with this type of self-knowledge that we can develop and grow as human beings. This self-knowledge is a major part of the honesty which I am advocating as the key element of developing a robust relationship with God. Nonetheless, an over-development of scrupulousness can be just as damaging as failing to acknowledge our weaknesses.

What then is an examination of consciousness? In the 1970s popular literature about *The Spiritual Exercises* began to emerge. In amongst this was a redrafting of the examen by

George Aschenbrenner SJ. In this version[14], whilst an examination of sinfulness was included, equal weight was given
to an examination of God's presence in our lives. The key
question is no longer simply: 'Where have I failed God?', but,
rather: 'Where have I been aware of God?'.

Why is this second question so important? It is worth re-
calling the Pelagian heresy, which claimed that salvation was
possible by the leading of a righteous life. The implication of
this is that God and, more specifically, the incarnation and
Paschal mystery are useful, but not necessary. It means that
the core of salvation is not relationship with God, but our capacity not to sin. Look at the two foci of the examen: we look
to our sinfulness and we look to where we have been aware
of God's presence. This second focus is absolutely crucial in
developing relationship with God. It is relationship with God
that facilitates salvation, regardless of one's sinfulness. It
does not matter whether I have gone to church every day,
and worked at a homeless shelter and adopted Aids orphans,
or whether I have led a far less wholesome life, far less fruitful life. If I have relationship with God, I have salvation. It is,
of course, true that to have any real relationship with God
without some attempt to live in a way that is not destructive of myself – or of those who interact with me – is almost
impossible. Hence the focus on my sinfulness remains important; it has relevance in deepening and developing my
self-awareness and my relationship with God.

I have chosen to emphasise this point because I think the
Pelagian heresy is alive and well and active in Christian
churches across the globe. I heard a sermon some time ago
where we were encouraged to focus on the religious significance of Christmas. We were told to raise this awareness in
ourselves by trying to improve our behaviour: by being more
patient, more charitable, and so on. Sadly, the preacher failed
to encourage us to notice God's presence. This is what I mean
when I say Pelagianism is alive and well. We are continually

---

14   George Aschenbrenner (2007).

taught to strive to be better, but we are rarely encouraged to notice that God is right alongside us in the daily chaos – or monotony – of our lives. God is present already; we do not have to change; we do not have to try harder; we do not have to do better. God is present. If we can truly focus our attention on God, the rest of the stuff will – perhaps only slowly – begin to move in a better direction. Given my own continual struggles with the 'same old' things, I find it enormously encouraging to know that God is not waiting for me to change before God gets involved!

Perhaps a helpful way of looking at this is to use a folk tale. A young native American boy was being put to bed by his grandfather. The boy turned to his grandfather and said 'Tell me the story of the two wolves.' The grandfather answered: 'In each person there are two wolves. One wolf is the joy, the laughter, the love, the life. The other wolf is destruction, corruption, anger and contempt. Each day these two wolves fight each other, each wolf trying to win the soul of the person.' The little boy thought for a while and then said, 'But Grandfather, which wolf wins?' The answer was simple: 'The one that you feed.'

The purpose of this story in this context is simply to say that by focusing merely on trying to eradicate your sinfulness you do not necessarily develop relationship with God. But developing relationship with God may well help in diminishing the power of some of the more malevolent voices in your head. I believe the real purpose of the examen is to give me a way to recognise where God is at work in my life, and therefore to 'feed that wolf', because, ultimately, that is the wolf that matters.

So how do I recognise the presence of God in my life? We may have particular memories where the presence of God seems absolutely indisputable. I remember one occasion at Mass in a small chapel in Livingstone House at Rhodes University. I had such a strong sense of the presence of the Spirit – it was almost tangible. I felt myself surrounded by God's presence.

This was a long time ago and it certainly has happened to me many times since then, but that was a very special moment. Oftentimes though, in daily life, the tangible sense of God's presence can be more elusive. Most often, this recognition of God's presence is simple: as simple as a moment of joy, a moment of feeling loved, a moment of loving, a moment of peace, a moment of beauty, an unexpected smile, a sense of connection. The things that touch me, the things that speak to me of God may be different from the things that speak to you. Nevertheless, there is frequently a familiarity of experience between people, and it is possible to recognise God at work in another person. Feelings associated with such experiences are peace, joy, life, energy, rootedness, connectedness, calmness; a sense of being loved, understood, cherished. And it is these kinds of feelings, evoked through ordinary experiences, which lead us to recognising God's presence in our lives. God often communicates in very ordinary ways. It worth remembering Teresa of Avila's words: 'You have no hands but ours; no feet but ours.' God connects with us through our connection with other people, with nature, with life, with music, with beauty.

The examen itself is one of the simplest of prayer formulations. It comprises three key features:

- Noticing where I have sinned or got in the way of God's grace.

- Noticing where God's presence has been.

- Talking to God about what I have noticed.

There are many versions of the examen and, as a result, it is easy to fall into the trap of wondering whether or not I am doing it 'correctly'. The key point to remember is simply this: if by practising the examen you find that you are becoming more aware of God's presence in your life, you are doing it correctly.

Use of the imagination in prayer

Another of the important prayer practices which has come down through the Ignatian tradition is the use of the imagination in prayer. Ignatian spirituality is a 'cataphatic' spirituality – that is to say, Ignatian spirituality uses images and lived experience as a way into encounter with God. Imagining how Jesus interacted with particular people, or actively engaging the imagination in a conversation with God is promoted. This is in stark contrast to the 'apophatic' or imageless way of prayer. In this second form of prayer all images, thoughts, ideas are set aside because they are inadequate: no image or thought or idea can capture the essence of God. Often, in apophatic prayer, the use of a mantra or focusing on breathing (or some other technique) is used to still the mind. Ideas, thoughts, images are noticed and then set aside. I do not believe that one way is superior to the other. Both apophatic and cataphatic prayer are found in the Christian tradition, and many people have found a deep and transformative encounter with God through both routes. In some cases one route seems to give way to the other as the prayer journey continues. It is important though to recognise which kind of prayer suits you best at the present moment, and it may be useful to know which traditions offer which methods. Nevertheless, I frequently found, during the years I spent working as a retreat director, that many people reject imaginative prayer before giving it a real chance. With a little encouragement, these same people found imaginative prayer fruitful.

So how do we use the imagination in prayer? In *The Spiritual Exercises*, St Ignatius delineates two ways. Firstly, imaginative contemplation, often referred to as 'Ignatian prayer'. In this type of prayer a scripture passage is used as a foundation. Gospel stories tend to lend themselves well to this type of prayer – there are lots of characters and there is interaction between different characters. In imaginative contemplation, the person who is praying is asked to take some time to set the scene in their mind. Take, for example, the story of

Bartimaeus, the blind beggar whom Jesus heals on his way out of Jericho[15]. You are invited, in your prayer, to imagine the road leading out of Jericho, to take time to notice whether it is sunny or not, to notice the people milling around, the camels, the goats, the smell of the dust and the animals, to see what people are wearing and to notice conversations. You are invited to picture Bartimaeus, and ultimately to take your place in the scene yourself, by imagining you are one of the characters you know was there. In using this particular story it is fairly common for people to take the place of Bartimaeus, although you could also be an apostle or a bystander. You then let the scene unfold: Jesus and disciples are leaving the city, Bartimaeus begins calling out, people tell him to be quiet, but he calls out again. Jesus beckons and asks Bartimaeus what he wants; to which Bartimaeus replies 'I want to see.' Jesus heals him and Bartimaeus follows Jesus along the road. A key question in the story is that Jesus asks Bartimaeus what he wants. As the scene unfolds, those praying find themselves caught up in the story; sometimes surprised by their own responses. At the end, once the story has played through, you take time to talk to Jesus. In Ignatian terms, this conversation is called the 'colloquy': Talking to Jesus as one friend talks to another.

The crucial component in this type of prayer is that it allows us to begin to see Jesus less as a mythical figure, and more as a person. It gives us a way of putting flesh on Jesus, as it were. It is important to dispel the idea of 'imagination' that is used when we talk of children having imaginary friends – the notion that the imagination is the realm of the unreal. Scientifically, the imagination is far more than this. It is the interface between our brains and the external environment. For example, imagination is crucial in the way in which we relate to other people. If a friend tells us about a particular interaction or occurrence in their lives, as well as making a mental picture of what they're describing, we use a combination of

---

15   Mark 10: 46–52.

memory and imagination to 'read' their facial expression and tone of voice in order to respond appropriately. Empathy is the capacity to blend our own life experience with the information we are being given through our imagination, and to respond appropriately with a felt sense of how it might be for that person in that context.

Imaginative prayer uses this faculty of the imagination. It allows us, for example, to blend our experience with the scripture reading, bringing to life a three-dimensional, responsive, reactive Jesus. It is to this three-dimensional, responsive, reactive – living – Jesus that we begin to relate. Although we are encouraged in the Christian tradition to have a relationship with God, most of us find it quite hard to relate to a 'mere' concept, a notion, an idea – a mystery. Imaginative prayer gives us an entry point into relationship; we have a Jesus who is alive.

A brief word of caution: it is worth taking a few moments, once your formal prayer is over, to examine what has happened in that prayer. To notice whether you are feeling more agitated, or less so, to notice whether the Jesus of your prayer is consistent with the Jesus proclaimed by the church, and found in the Gospels. This is not to say that anything that is inconsistent with church teaching should immediately be discarded, but rather that it can be a useful lodestone. The use of imagination is powerful, but not without risk. It is well worth while to apply some discernment to your prayer. (Discernment is dealt with in more detail in later chapters – in particular in Chapter 6.)

Imaginative contemplation is the most obvious way in which Ignatius encourages the use of the imagination in prayer. However, there is a small, often overlooked, paragraph in *The Spiritual Exercises*[16] which focuses the entire prayer period towards God, regardless of the content of the prayer. Ignatius

---

16   Paragraph 75 – the third additional note given at the end of the material on the First Week.

suggests some additions 'for making the Exercises better and for finding more readily what one wants'. One of these 'additions' goes like this: a step or two before the place where I will pray, I will stand for the space of an Our Father and consider how God is looking at me.

I will pause just before entering my place of prayer and consider how God is looking at me. The significance of this is substantial. Firstly, it is clear that Ignatius expects that we will find God there. Secondly, we are not simply asked to feel God's presence, but we are encouraged to consider *how God is looking at us*. The underlying premise is that God is responsive. We are to expect that the way in which God is looking at us is likely to change from day to day, from prayer period to prayer period. This is precisely because each day, as we engage in prayer, we are a little different. Some days we are excited, joyful and filled with gratitude, other days we may be struggling to overcome anger, or feelings of gross injustice. God notices how we are and responds to us in that place.

It is probably worth noting here that, whilst some people do 'see an expression on God's face' in their mind's eye, most of us will simply experience a sense of the quality of that expression. We will know whether God is smiling, or looking thoughtful, whether God is concerned or amused.

It is this 'noticing of God's expression' which sets the scene for the rest of the Ignatian prayer period. We begin with an act of the imagination, a noticing and an interpreting. This sets us up for the dialoguing with God as one friend talks to another which will form a substantial part of the prayer period.

Lectio divina

Lectio divina means 'sacred reading'. It had its origin in the ancient monasteries: the practice is mentioned in the Rule of St Benedict which dates from the early sixth century. In the monastery there would be only one Bible. As the community gathered for prayer, a biblical passage would be read aloud several times. Each monk would then focus on a particular short section of the passage which had struck him, and ruminate on that section while he went about his daily work. Nowadays, the practice is widely used in private prayer by people across the Christian denominations. In essence, this prayer begins with asking God to reveal what God wishes to reveal through the Bible passage. Then the passage is slowly read, more than once, until a particular word, phrase or sentence jumps out. The person praying then spends time slowly digesting the essence of this fragment, talking to God about it and listening for God's response. This process may be repeated several times. *Lectio divina* is most commonly applied to scripture, but it is also applicable to any short passage or poem with a spiritual flavour.

The practice of prayer

There are phases in our lives when making time for formal prayer may be extremely difficult. The most obvious example is being parents with young children. Many people in such circumstances find their lack of ability to find the prayer time they enjoyed as a young single adult enormously frustrating. It is important to recognise the real limitations imposed by the conditions of your life, and simply to accept that, and do what you can. Nonetheless, there is little doubt that investing in formal prayer time makes a substantial difference in your life. Sheila Cassidy in *Prayer for Pilgrims*[17] writes of the importance of the backbone of formal prayer in our daily lives, precisely because it increases our awareness of the presence of God in the moment. She gives a simple example of seeing the image of the cross in the wooden strips of a window. Cassidy then talks about the well-known phenomenon of seeing something beautiful and immediately wanting to share the

---

17   Sheila Cassidy (1982).

experience with someone we are close to. Always the person with whom we want to share our emotion is someone with whom we actively communicate – very probably on a daily basis. Similarly, she says, with prayer: we are more likely to be mindful of God's presence in our daily activities if we have a regular formal prayer period or 'quiet time'.

Reading spiritual material

Reading spiritual material is an important practice in supporting a healthy faith life. Traditionally this applies to material which is explicitly about faith. It helps because you can feel reassurance if you read about someone else's experience which is similar to your own. So, in reading about other people's experience, your thoughts can be expanded, or perhaps endorsed.

Many of the classical texts of spirituality, though well worth reading, can be a little inaccessible, particularly to someone who is exploring this territory for the first time. There are, however, many excellent contemporary authors. Among my favourites are William Barry SJ, Margaret Silf and Richard Rohr OFM. The book you have in your hands would also constitute spiritual reading. There is a great deal of poetry which can also be used in this way – or can even be used a little more formally in *lectio divina*.

Ideally, reading spiritual material should provide food for thought. And, whilst there are multitudes of programs available for people starting out on the Christian walk, there are relatively few designed for those already fairly well schooled in the basics of their faith. So reading spiritual material is a great way to further your own faith education. Many books are also available in audio format, so 'reading' can also be done this way – perhaps during the daily bus or train commute to and from work. Other forms of spiritual input such as short talks, sermons, or webcasts can also be used in this way.

Conclusion

I firmly believe in the importance of investing time in a healthy, vibrant prayer life. It will flourish in the same way that human relationships flourish when we spend time together. And if you have slipped out of the habit, remember that, just as old friends can pick up a conversation after many months or years of silence, so too we can pick up the conversation with God at any time. There are just two important points:

- God is waiting for you when you pray.

- Honesty is the gateway to a real, dynamic prayer life.

There are, of course, 'dark night of the soul' experiences, but I think many of us mistake our own ability to hide from ourselves for dryness in prayer. The dark night of the soul is characterised by a longing for God: a profound and unquenchable thirst for God. For most of us, the aridity we sometimes experience in prayer will probably come from some inner transition we have not yet noticed and come to terms with – or perhaps simply from lack of attention.

Why do you pray?

What is the fruit of prayer in your life?

How is God looking at you?

What kind of prayer is actually working for you at the moment?

You may find it helpful to return to these questions from time to time.

Chapter 4: Desire

Where is the Life we have lost in the living?
—*TS Eliot*

This chapter is titled 'Desire'. Notice your response to the word 'desire'. What does it mean to you? What does it mean to you in a faith context? For many of us, desire is simply not a word we associate with faith. It is something to be mildly suspicious of; something to back away from. Regardless of our attitudes towards it, desire is a force that is operative in our lives. It affects the way in which we spend our time, and who we spend our time with. It influences the hobbies we choose to pursue and the careers we follow. It shapes the way we choose to pray and worship.

··

In the previous chapter I mentioned the apophatic and cataphatic traditions of prayer. Although these paths to prayer are very different, both can lead one deeper in the mystery of God. Likewise, in spirituality there are different approaches to human desire. The Buddhist approach teaches that desire is the root of all suffering: if we are able to let go of desire completely we will no longer suffer. In the Christian tradition the ascetic route is one of rigorous self denial in order to tame the lusts of the flesh. (Forgive the melodramatic flourish; it was too hard to resist!)

A good example of an ascetic is Teresa of Avila. Well known for her mysticism, she was also a reformer of the Carmelite order. The order had become rather lax in living out their vows of poverty. She set out to revive the strict set of rules laid down by the founders of the order, opting for absolute poverty – demonstrated, amongst other things, by being discalced (shoeless). The ascetic route affords a potentially powerful way into communion with God – provided of course, perfection in ascetism does not itself become the goal, rather than communion with God. That slippage can too easily occur: we get distracted by the process, and forget the purpose of our self-discipline.

Disordered desire

Ignatian spirituality, whilst upholding the value of ascetism, does not require the practice in quite the same way as Teresa did. The purpose of making the Spiritual Exercises is 'to overcome oneself, and to order one's life without reaching a decision through some disordered affection[18]'. In some ways it doesn't sound very different from the ascetic route since the phrase 'overcoming oneself' has strong undertones of self denial. But notice the last phrase: 'through some disordered affection'. The problem for Ignatius is not desire itself, but disordered desire.

This idea of disordered desire is probably best illustrated through Ignatius' own life[19]. Ignatius was converted from being an ambitious young 'wannabe' courtier to an ardent follower of Christ during a long period of convalescence after being wounded in battle. When he had recovered, he left his home in Loyola and travelled to a famous Benedictine monastery at Montserrat where he prepared for a full confession and spent a night in vigil before the Black Madonna. At the end of this night Ignatius laid down his sword before

---

18   Ganss (1992) The Spiritual Exercises of St Ignatius of Loyola [22]. By convention, quotations from The Spiritual Exercises are given as paragraphs rather than page numbers – for consistency between translations.

19   The novel Just call me López by Margaret Silf (2012) gives a delightful look into the life of Ignatius of Loyola.

the statue as a symbol of the change in his life's direction. He also left his mule and the clothing of a nobleman at the monastery and proceeded to the town of Manresa in the dress of a beggar, on the start of a pilgrimage to Jerusalem. He had planned to spend only a few days at Manresa, but ended staying almost a year. He spent his time there in prayer, doing penance, serving the poor and the sick, and speaking to ordinary people. During this time he was increasingly beset by scruples. He was plagued by memories of his former life that he feared he had not confessed adequately, and so he made confession after confession to try to ensure that he was truly absolved. He did not cut his hair or his nails and slowly but surely, in his attempt to live a truly ascetic life, he fell into what we might now recognise as a deep depression. He seriously contemplated taking his own life, and it was only at this point that he was able to recognise the destructive trajectory he was taking and was able to choose a more moderate version of the life of a pilgrim.

Ignatius' desire to live an exceptional life as an ascetic was a disordered desire. It was potentially a good desire, and one that could have led him into deeper relationship with God. But the desire was driven by Ignatius' ambition, rather than by God's invitation. His conversion had occurred during a time of convalescence. On his sick bed he had imagined himself outdoing the practices of the great saints. It was this daydreaming which had brought about his conversion, but the living out of this dream almost caused his demise. Was Ignatius wrong to follow this desire? I do not – cannot – know, nor do I think that it is particularly useful to judge the pursuit of particular desires in this way. Even though his pursuit of this desire had a destructive trajectory, with some reflection Ignatius was able to use the experience in shaping his own view of world, and this later provided a useful insight in the development of *The Spiritual Exercises*. This is another way of saying God was able to use this negative-seeming experience for God's own ends, and to allow Ignatius to find value in the experience. Nevertheless the single-minded pursuit of this route very nearly cost Ignatius his life.

For Ignatius then, noticing one's desires and being discerning in one's choices is an essential part of the journey towards God. As I have already remarked, the fundamental premise here is that it is not desire itself that is the problem, but, rather, disordered desire. Feeling desire is a part of what it is to be human, and to have a spirituality which allows us to take that seriously, and to use that as a way into encounter with God, somehow fits.

Living deliberately

To approach this idea from a different angle, one of the great ideas that has helped to shape my adult life is the idea of living deliberately. For the last fifteen years or so, I have been trying to live deliberately. I have no desire to be swept along by trends and movements and external events. I have wanted to actively choose my life path as much as I can. (This idea has, of course, has been built on the foundation of a loving, stable family and a good solid education.)

The phrase 'to live deliberately' comes from Henry David Thoreau's *Walden*.

> I went to the woods because I wished to live deliberately, to front only the essential facts of life, and see if I could not learn what it had to teach, and not, when I came to die, discover that I had not truly lived[20].

I do not necessarily agree with Thoreau's philosophy as a whole but this quotation touches something deep within me – I find a deep stirring, a longing, a desire to LIVE. Like many of my generation, I was first exposed to this quotation through the film *Dead Poets' Society*. The film, set in the 1950s, tells the story of an inspirational English teacher at a conservative, but highly respected school. He shares these

---

20   Henry David Thoreau (1997) p.66.

words from *Walden* with a group of final year high school boys. The film follows the development of the young men as they begin to pay attention to their dreams, and choose to follow their passions. It is a powerful and tragic film, illustrating that following one's passion is not always simple and may come at great cost.

In the world today, there seems to be a great deal of talk about the pursuit of one's dreams, but surprisingly little talk of discernment. Good discernment is possible only in a context in which deep reflection is valued and nurtured, and yet we live in a world that seems to thrive on distraction. Ignatius would be deeply suspicious of the kind of self-centred pursuit of happiness which is so widely promoted under the guise of 'purpose'. The same kind of questioning echoes in TS Eliot's *The Rock*[21]:

> The endless cycle of idea and action,
> Endless invention, endless experiment,
> Brings knowledge of motion, but not of stillness;
> Knowledge of speech, but not of silence;
> Knowledge of words, and ignorance of the Word.
> All our knowledge brings us nearer to our ignorance,
> All our ignorance brings us nearer to death,
> But nearness to death no nearer to GOD.
> Where is the Life we have lost in living?
> Where is the wisdom we have lost in knowledge?
> Where is the knowledge we have lost in information?
> The cycles of Heaven in twenty centuries
> Bring us farther from GOD and nearer to the Dust.

To live deliberately means actively choosing, and actively choosing means paying attention to the things that stir within us. It requires that we notice the desires that contin-

---

21   TS Eliot (1974) p.155.

ually ebb and flow in our being, and which spring from no-where and quickly fade. It requires patience and attendance. It requires self-knowledge.

Ways to view desire

It is important to recognise at the outset that the Christian tradition often teaches us to be deeply suspicious of desire. Desire is seen as something to be ignored, driven from our minds, suppressed. We are to act as we ought to act, not as we desire to act. The underlying presumption is that our desires will lead us to a dark and depraved space. Add a cursory knowledge of Freudian psychoanalysis into the mix, and desires are seen to be truly dangerous and nasty, forces to be rooted out at all costs. The image of the ascetic hermit fighting hideous internal forces of desire with the use of tortuous devices called 'disciplines' is a real part of our history. At the heart of the problem is the reduction of the meaning of the word 'desire' to mean simply 'lust'. From the perspective of the institutional church, it is fairly easy to understand why desire is treated with suspicion, and indeed why the Principle and Foundation of Ignatian spirituality may be a little challenging:

> All the things in this world are a gift of God, presented to us so that we can know God more easily...Our only desire and our own choice should be this: I want and choose what better leads to God's deepening his life in me.

In a world where all things can, potentially, lead us into encounter with God, the guiding force should be an informed and active conscience, rather than a set of rules. Herein lies the problem. Firstly, the world is not black and white. It is not really possible to teach that there is an objective right and wrong. This is not to say that nothing can be categorised in this way, but even the taking of a person's life has different names in different contexts: Murder is not the same as manslaughter, and self-defence and assisted suicide are something else again. So even things such as the taking of a life, which might at first glance appear to be black and white – indisputably right or wrong – have different meanings in different contexts. It is far easier for the Church to teach 'right' and 'wrong' in terms of absolutes. It is also far easier to teach the concepts of right and wrong in the abstract rather than the particular. This is not to say that standards are not important, but simply to acknowledge that most of us live our daily reality in a greyscale world where right and wrong are relative rather than absolute.

Furthermore, for most people who are trying to live a life of faith and integrity, many of the choices we have to make are between what is the good, and what is the better. It is not about some intrinsic quality of the thing chosen, but about the appropriateness of that thing in my life – my life here, now. Precisely because the pursuit of faith gives us the capacity to distinguish, we seldom have trouble recognising the difference between right and wrong – it is far more useful to examine how we can distinguish between the good and the better. It is important to understand that 'good' and 'better' are not objective categories; that we need to be discerning. If two people are faced with choosing between the same two things, the better choice for the first person may not necessarily be the better choice for the second.

Another reason that the institutional Church may view desire with suspicion is that it fails to distinguish between two types of desire: hedonic desire and eudaemonic desire. This distinction dates back to the ancient Greeks and is at the heart of Aristotelian ethics. The goal of a hedonic life is pleasure – we see this concept in the more common English word 'hedonism'. It is hedonic desire that is manipulated by the advertising industry. Buy this car, this perfume, this pair of shoes and you will be happy, popular, and so on. The purchase of the new item does give a feeling of satisfaction and pleasure, but it wears off and as it does we begin to look for the next hedonic hit. It is this kind of desire of which the church is appropriately suspicious. Eudaemonic[22] desire is something different. Eudaemonism is the belief that a good life is one that is characterised by living according to one's virtues. Put in this way, it may sound a little unappealing. A more helpful expression may be that eudaemonic desire is a desire for meaning and purpose in life. Achieving the object of eudaemonic desire usually does not result in the kind of pleasure hit that we associate with hedonic pleasure, but it can, and frequently does, lead to a robust sense of contentment and well-being. As Victor Frankl puts it in his influential book *Man's Search for Meaning*: 'Happiness cannot be pursued: it must ensue. One must have a reason to be happy. Once the reason is found, however, one becomes happy automatically[23].'

Considering extrinsic and intrinsic motivation is also a useful way into understanding desire. Extrinsic motivations are directed primarily towards external praise, reward or affirmation. Extrinsic motivation is the driving force behind consumer culture. It manifests itself as the pursuit of money, possessions and status. It is the construction of the 'perfect' persona – to achieve social integration at the level to which one aspires. Seen in this stark light, it may be easy to dismiss extrinsic motivation as not being problematic. The fact that you are reading this book suggests that you are aware of the importance of eudaemonic desire. But consider your response to praise, for example. Do you crave recognition for the job that you do? There is an ongoing conversation, for example, over the merits of stay-at-home mothers versus working mothers. The conversation can get pretty heated and totally polarised. But the truth is that being a parent in either situation is incredibly hard work and has no extrinsic reward. Society does not formally reward good parenting in

---

22   Greek: eu – good, happily; daimon – guardian, guiding spirit (hence eudaimonia – happiness).

23   Victor Frankl (2006) In 'Preface to the 1992 edition'.

any way. Similarly, at universities across the world there is an ongoing tension in that research is extrinsically rewarded, whereas teaching is not. Most institutions will say that they value both teaching and research equally. The difficulty is that teaching has the same extrinsic value to the institution whether it is performed excellently or poorly, but the quality of research is more closely correlated with the way in which the university generates income. As a result, those academics who spend more time focused on research will tend to gain more recognition from the university and may well receive financial reward for their efforts.

Just to give a bit of perspective, however, it is important to recognise at least one of the reasons why we (as society) are where we are at the moment. The over-emphasis in our time of the importance of extrinsic values is not all bad. A century ago, for example, the class divide was incredibly powerful. It did not matter how much money you had, if you weren't born into the right family, you weren't acceptable. The system was built on attributes over which you had no control. Nowadays, that is not true; many of our role models have come from very humble beginnings. The shift to recognising extrinsic qualities has been useful in breaking down the strong class divide. Nonetheless, as ever in human life, the pendulum has swung too far in the other direction. There are many examples of people who have made huge amounts of money, or who are famous, but who inspire little respect.

Extrinsic rewards are really possible only for measurable contributions. This results in a skewing: only those things which can be extrinsically rewarded are seen to be valuable. For example, people have argued that stay-at-home mothers should be paid. The problem is not that the work they do has little value, but rather that we have created a system where we recognise extrinsic reward as being the only 'real' reward. Perhaps an opportunity which could emerge out of the massive financial crisis of recent years would be finding a way to value intrinsic rewards as a society.

Intrinsic goals are those which are focused on finding meaning and purpose in life, personal growth and the development of good relationships. None of these things can be bought; they all require time, effort and intentional engagement. The pursuit of these things can itself bring a sense of pleasure and well-being. This wholesomeness often takes a long time to develop and grow, but once it is present, it is surprisingly persistent. It can sustain itself, even when external circumstances are challenging. It is also surprisingly satisfying.

Once again, in examining our motivations, it is crucial to be honest with ourselves. The pursuit of things which are good in themselves, for example taking care of the poor and marginalised, can be done mainly – or at least in part – for extrinsic rewards. The moment you find yourself wondering 'what will people think?', or looking for some kind of recognition for what you are doing, your motivation is, at least in part, extrinsic. Some years ago I made a decision to leave full-time ministry working at a Jesuit retreat house and return to a postdoctoral fellowship in chemistry. Although it was fairly clear to me that the choice was a good one, I couldn't help but wonder what people would think about the choice I was making. To leave a job which seemed more meaningful or 'holy' to return to something secular was not an obvious 'good' choice in the context of a religious community. As I sat with that discomfort, I realised that my real challenge was not so much with 'other people', but coming to reconcile my choice in terms of my image of myself. I was no longer one who gave up the potential of a successful career in chemistry to pursue God. I was once again an 'ordinary' Christian. That took some living into!

Sifting desires

It is this sifting between extrinsic and intrinsic motivation and eudaemonic and hedonic desire which is at the heart of Ignatian spirituality. In the Principle and Foundation, Ignatius writes:

Consequently, on our own part we ought not to seek health rather than sickness, wealth rather than poverty, honor rather than dishonor, a long life rather than a short one, and so on in all other matters. Rather, we ought to desire and choose only that which is more conducive to the end for which we are created.[24]

The reason for this is not that it is a bad thing to be honoured, or to have wealth, or to live a long life. Rather it is that all of those things are extrinsic motivations not intrinsic ones. The end for which we are created can be understood as finding meaning; finding our unique place in the world; making the contribution that only we are able to make. Nonetheless, it is important that we do not get too upset with ourselves when we discover that our motivations for doing the good and noble thing that we have chosen to pursue are laced with a desire for recognition of some sort. If we wait to act or choose until we have the perfect pure intrinsic motivation we will never act. As Richard Rohr puts it, drawing from Plato: 'We need to live our way into a new way of thinking rather than to think our way into a new way of living.' Thus we need to focus on choosing between the good and the better, not from an external point of view, but from what is stirring within us at a given time.

While I was doing my doctorate, my parish priest invited me to consider taking on a formal part-time role in the parish with a focus on the youth. At the time, I had just finished making the Spiritual Exercises and I was looking for an outlet for my enthusiasm for spirituality. But as I sat with the choice, I realised I would be doing it only because it seemed like a good thing to do, not because it seemed like the right thing for me to do at that time. It

---

24   The Spiritual Exercises of St Ignatius of Loyola [23]. (I have intentionally used a slightly different translation here.)

seemed better at the time to focus my energy on finishing my doctorate, which would then give me freedom to pursue what I felt called to do. Working for the parish would have been a good thing, and I am sure many people would have benefitted from my involvement. But for me, the better thing was to focus on my research. (A few years later a different solution emerged for the parish, which in the long run has probably been better for the parish too.)

Mimetic desire

In the context of desire, one further idea to consider is that of 'mimetic' ("mimicking") desire. This is described in the work of twentieth century French historian, literary critic, and philosopher René Girard. Author Gil Bailie, commenting on Girard's work, writes 'Desire, as distinguished from animal appetite, is always aroused by the desire of another; we desire what the other desires[25]'. I find this a powerful idea. The example most frequently given to illustrate this point is that of two toddlers playing in a room with many toys, who will almost always end up fighting over a single toy. As one child observes the other enjoying playing with some particular toy he will want to play with it too. As the child who has the toy observes the other's desire for the toy, she realises that she has an object that is desirable and so is more reluctant to let it go. As much as we like to believe in our autonomy and individuality, it seems that we desire most of what we desire because we observe those around us pursuing or enjoying those things. Again, this is the driving force behind most advertising. We are shown images of happy, smiling people using some product and a part of us automatically responds to that. There is a great deal more to Girard's work, but his concept of mimetic desire is useful in helping us understand how our desires operate.

---

25   Gil Bailie (1999) pp.134–153.

It is usually easier to observe effects in others than to recognise them in ourselves. For instance if we consider the influence that a circle of friends can have on someone we know well, we can often see a dynamic of mimetic desire in play – the manner in which they choose to spend their time, or the things they choose to prioritise may be strongly influenced by their companions at any given time. It is important then for each of us to realise that we ourselves are similarly influenced: we need to spend time alone, considering what we truly value, the kind of life we wish to lead, and then to seek out the companionship of those who have similar values and goals.

Dealing with desire

At the heart of any spirituality which takes desire seriously, there must be a strong emphasis on self-awareness. We need to pay close attention to the subtle movements that take place within us. We need to notice the influence of different people in our lives. We need to be able to distinguish between hedonic and eudaemonic desire, and be honest with ourselves about our need for extrinsic as well as intrinsic rewards. We need to be conscious of the way in which we interact with the world, and about the things which are life-giving to us. We need to know where we are, internally, at any given time, and whether we are able to take on a particular challenge at that particular point. The same person may be faced with the same decision at two different points in time and make different choices – and both can be the better choice. I will illustrate this at some length from my personal experience.

In 2008, I applied for a job as an academic in the Chemistry Department at Stellenbosch University. There was a line in the advertisement requiring the applicant to be fluent in Afrikaans. I have very little Afrikaans but I applied for the job anyway. After some months I hadn't heard from the university and had started investigating the possibility of doing a postdoc[26] in the United States. At the time, I wanted a job in chemistry, but I was still struggling with viewing myself as an academic – I believed that in order to do that job to the best of my ability I would have to ignore the side of myself which was passionate about spirituality. I was also very unsure of my ability to be an academic. For some reason (probably the requirement for Afrikaans) there were very few applicants for the job. The Chemistry Department seemed to be fairly desperate at the time, and when the Head of Department heard that I was thinking of going overseas he called me in and said that they really did want to employ me, but they would need to re-advertise the post without the Afrikaans requirement in order to be able to appoint me. It was made quite clear that if I wanted the job it was mine for the taking. I thought about it for a while, and then politely declined. In 2009, almost exactly a year later, the same department advertised another position. This time I applied and I was delighted when I was appointed.

Both choices were the right choices. So what had changed? The year that passed between those two decisions was pivotal. Essentially what shifted is that I found a way in which I could create personal meaning within an academic career. This happened through an unexpected route. Instead of doing a postdoc in medicinal chemistry in the USA (where I had a firm offer from a research group at Boston University), I chose to do a postdoc in science education in Cape Town. It was a very risky move. In fact, when I began the education postdoc, I wasn't even sure that I was going to get funding for the year. I had enough money saved to be able to support myself for about a year, and I believed that the postdoc was the right thing to do. (As it turned out, my postdoc supervisor did manage to get me funding.)

---

26   'A postdoc' is shorthand for a postdoctoral research fellowship. It is a period of intensive research, usually at a university, and usually lasting 1 to 2 years. It is common for scientists to have held several postdocs before securing a permanent position.

Importantly, as I began to read education literature I came across ideas which had echoes in spirituality – perhaps most significantly the value of the 'being' of the student. In reading, researching and writing in education I began to believe in my own ability to make a meaningful contribution to the world through academia. I had known that I was capable of making a contribution through medicinal chemistry but I couldn't make the internal leap to believing that I could make a *meaningful* contribution[27].

This last point is important; this question is at the heart of the discernment process, the sifting of desires. When we need to choose between two things which are both good or have value to society, the focus of the question becomes what happens internally when I interact with these two things. The better choice will be the one which gives me access to greater meaning (more on this later). It is interesting for me to recognise that in discovering the meaning of my contribution to science education, I began to see elements of meaning in my medicinal chemistry research. So in starting my academic career I was trying to balance both aspects.

The first time I applied for the job at Stellenbosch I hadn't yet made the connection between my academic career and a personal sense of meaning. The second time, I had found that meaning. The fact that I didn't embark on my academic career until I'd found that sense of meaning made the transition into the role much easier for me. I do not look for affirmation or approval as I would have done before my perspective shifted. I find it much easier to navigate my way through this strange world – because I have found my intrinsic motivation.

Taking desire seriously has led me to a much more fruitful life. It has also led me to creating a life which I love. Follow-

---

27   Please note that this is not to say that I believed a contribution to the science of medicinal chemistry inherently lacked meaning. It was simply that I was struggling to make the connection to meaning for myself.

ing the internal sense of what seemed right on all major decisions has served me incredibly well. I trust my ability to see what is going on around me, and I trust my capacity to choose a path that is life giving.

But it's important to say that it has taken me a long time to 'train myself' into noticing and using my desires constructively. Spiritual direction was my first real training ground, and in more recent years I've found that I can use conversations with particular friends as well. This requires a good deal of self-knowledge and a commitment to honesty with myself, and with those to whom I talk.

Some tools

It should be clear by now that one of the recurring themes of this book is the importance of honesty with oneself. The capacity for honesty is greatly enhanced by reflection and by an ability to recognise the qualitative difference between interior pushes and pulls – to use Ignatian terms: the movements which occur within us.

Research that is currently emerging on post traumatic growth shows that there are a number of factors which increase the probability of emotional growth after a substantial traumatic event. One of these factors is sometimes called 'emotional granularity'. This is the capacity to distinguish between closely related emotions – for example to be able to notice the difference between joy and happiness, between grief and sorrow, between anger and rage. As my brother-in-law, Phil, puts it: a low level of emotional granularity is akin to having my first pack of crayons – eight bold colours; while a high level is akin to having a box with the full range of a hundred and twenty colours. The difference between burnt orange and burnt sienna, or between pink flamingo and pink sherbet, is simply not available when one has only a choice of orange and pink.

It has been reported[28] that traumatised people who are able distinguish between subtle differences in experienced emotion are usually more able to respond constructively once the initial shock of trauma has worn off – precisely because they are more aware of what they are actually experiencing. I should add that it is probably more important for the person to be able to distinguish between their different emotions than for them to be able to label the emotion accurately. For example, during the conversation I had with Phil on emotional granularity, we realised that we use the words 'happiness' and 'joy' to describe different emotional experiences, but we were both clear on the emotional experiences we were trying to describe.

I think that emotional granularity is closely correlated with our ability to reflect. However, reflection alone is not sufficient for a high level of emotional granularity. It also requires an ability to notice the emotional content of our experience. Whilst I am now able to notice, identify and articulate my emotional experience with a high degree of precision, this was not always the case. I have always been a deeply reflective person, and when I first started to become interested in the ministry of spiritual direction I noticed that the question 'How do you feel?' was frequently asked. At the time I found it a very difficult question to answer. When someone asked me how I felt, it was not simply that I was not able to put a word on the feeling I was experiencing, it was also that I really had no idea what that 'feeling' was. It was as if I did not know how to access that information. This is not to say that I did not feel things, it was just that when I actively tried to pay attention to my feelings I seemed to be unable to focus. I discussed this with a spiritual director friend. She gave me a list of 'feeling words' and suggested that it might help me find language for my experience. Following that conversation, I began to teach myself how to name my feelings. As I started to pray each morning, I would choose three words

---

28   Michele Tugade, Barbara Fredrickson & Lisa Feldman Barrett (2004) pp.1161–1190.

that most closely seemed to resonate with how I was feeling at that time. After a few months I was able to name my feelings without having to look at the list, and after a few more months I was finally able to answer that kind of question when asked.

Honesty with ourselves requires that we pay close attention to our internal world, so that we are able to recognise the subtle shifts that occur over time. Knowing ourselves well is similar to knowing another person well. It is something that develops over time and requires daily attention. If we are not noticing the small shifts and changes as they happen, we will wake up one day and wonder what on earth became of our dreams and our desires. It is not the paying of attention to our desires that is the road to perdition; rather it is our failure to notice the subtle pulls and pushes, our failure to interrogate our motivations, that leads us to make choices blindly, and can result in a great deal of heartache and regret.

But paying attention to desire does not guarantee a smooth ride. Sometimes a path that looks promising turns out to be filled with unforeseen challenges. Life is not simple and things do go wrong. As Victor Frankl points out, we are far more likely to find lasting happiness if we seek meaning. We are living in an environment that favours extrinsic reward rather than meaning. If the theory is correct, mimetic desire makes it quite hard to focus on meaning in our lives. We will continually be drawn into seeking extrinsic rewards, precisely because everyone around us sees those as being attractive. We need to find communities of praxis: small groups of people who share our desire to live deliberately, to pay attention to desire and to consciously choose that which will bring intrinsic value to our lives. It is important for us to find others who are trying to live in this way, who can walk the walk beside us.

There is breath in my body
and blood in my veins.
Continuously, ceaselessly
my heart beats a rhythm
that is solely my own.
Life blood and oxygen carry out
their silent exchange.
Small molecules maintaining my existence.
Two words turn over
and over in my mind –
Choose Life!
But I did not choose to breathe
nor pace the gentle rhythm of my heart.
I did not choose the colour of my hair,
my eyes, my skin.
I did not choose where or when to be born.
So what then does it mean –
Choose Life!
Time will pass whether I use it or not.
The years will flow by whether I act and create
or whether I sit idly by.
My beating heart continues whether I reach for my dreams
or hide behind my fears.
To choose life is to dare to dream
and to risk failure,
to dare to love
and to risk rejection.
It is to see the waves;
to feel the wind on your face;
to taste the salt spray
and to risk stepping out of the boat.
Oh how I want to Choose Life[29]!

---

29   Margaret Blackie (2008) p.94.

Conclusion

It is often said that our deepest desire and God's desire for us are the same thing. When we think about desire in terms of eudaemonic desire, the deep thirst for meaning and purpose, the possibility that our desire and God's might be the same begins to seem possible. It also evident, with this understanding, that it is indeed possible for every person to find their place in our world; to find their unique contribution. The search for meaning and purpose does not rely on the availability of extrinsic resources in the same way as hedonic desire does.

Pause for a moment and notice what remains with you from this chapter.

Where is the gentle invitation?

Is there something in this approach which is attractive?

Who is the God who is present?

Notice too if you find yourself a little fearful.

Take some time to talk to God about the things that are stirring in you.

Chapter 5: Grace

This reality of God is communicated in what theology calls grace
and invites us to a totally trustful surrender of our own being
— Philip Endean SJ

Pause and call to mind moments of grace: Those experiences which inspire wonder. Moments in which we know something has changed inside us, but we aren't sure how it happened.

The way in which I most commonly experience this is when I have been mentally and emotionally struggling with some issue. There may be no change for a long time, but then something clicks or shifts or changes and I find myself viewing the issue differently. Many years ago I spent a few months battling with faith. I was living in France at the time and frequently visited Sacre Cœur. One day I found myself looking up at the great mosaic above the altar and discovered that I believed. It is these experiences which give us a glimpse into the action of grace.

Pause and take a few moments now to remember these kinds of experiences.

....

What is grace?

There is no easy way describe the experience that I am trying to access in this chapter. The difficulty lies in trying to grasp the most slippery of theological terms: grace. It is the only term that I am able to use to describe the experience I want to evoke, but at the same time the term 'grace' is understood and used in slightly different ways.

I will start with Karl Rahner's understanding of grace[30] – or perhaps more accurately, my understanding of Rahner's usage of the concept of grace. For Rahner, God's communication is accessible by every human being. It is unique and particular to each individual. It is something that is real and something that has the capacity to influence the human person fundamentally. This is grace. As I am using it here, grace is an effect that occurs as a result of active engagement with God. Of course I do not believe that grace is limited by our conscious accessing of God, as I believe God is far more generous than this understanding would allow. Nevertheless, in this section I am limiting the discussion to that which is consciously sought and which has a noticeable effect even if the effect is noticed only with hindsight. The point is simply this: that grace could be operating on a far greater scale than the occurrences of which we are consciously aware, but grace beyond our awareness cannot be discussed or exemplified in any meaningful way. It lies in the realm of unknown unknowns. As such it may impact our lives, but it is something beyond our conscious reality.

The idea of grace being something to pray for comes through in *The Spiritual Exercises*, where each Week has its own grace. Ignatius actively encourages the practice of praying explicitly for a particular grace: holding this desire before God at the beginning of each prayer period. In the context of making the Exercises, the grace sought is closely linked to both the material of the prayer and the overall dynamic of the Exercises. And indeed, from the viewpoint of the one praying, as well as from that of the spiritual director, it is evident that something has changed inside: the grace is beginning to take hold.

---

30   For an accessible entry into the writings of Karl Rahner, see *Karl Rahner: Spiritual Writings*, edited by Philip Endean (Karl Rahner, 2004).

Let's take the grace of the First Week as an example. This is to know oneself to be a loved sinner, and the prayer material of the First Week takes the exercitant through a conscious engagement with the love of God, followed by a series of exercises which reveal different aspects of the nature of sin, and the consequences of sin. As mentioned in Chapter 2, the dynamic of the First Week follows a particular pattern. It begins with a growing felt sense of the love of God – both in general terms and also, importantly, for me as an individual. Once that sense has begun to take root, there is a slight change of gear into the consideration of the nature of sin. Any level of engagement with the material will result in a realisation that I sin. Inevitably, I will begin to acknowledge, and to hold before God in prayer the painful truth that I participate in sin. Sometimes that participation is in full knowledge and with full intent, and with an acceptance of the consequences of my actions, but more often than not I participate in sin out of ignorance and a lack of appreciation of the bigger picture. So, as I sit in prayer with these two strong movements – initially that God loves me, followed by a consideration of who I am in my strengths and in my brokenness – I begin to realise that I am indeed a sinner and that I am as much in need of salvation (however we understand it) as anyone else. Sooner or later, it will become clear to me that God loves me as I am – *and* I am a sinner. To put it another way, as described by Richard Rohr: God does not love me because *I* am good, God loves me because *God* is good. In that movement I begin to see that unconditional love *is actually unconditional* and that this is the way that God loves me. I am indeed a loved sinner.

Praying for a particular grace is not simply something done while one is making the Exercises. It needs to be an important part of every day's prayer. When one considers the graces associated with making the Spiritual Exercises it is easy to overlook the importance of praying for grace in our daily lives. The graces can appear slightly stylised and not particularly applicable to daily reality. Certainly it has taken me the best part of twelve years working fairly constantly with the material for this particular penny to drop. There are, of course, other aspects of the Spiritual Exercises such as discernment, which are crucial to growing into maturity of love, of life and of faith. But learning to identify the grace which we need at a particular point in time, and then praying for it, is an indispensible tool for the life of faith.

Why is praying for a grace so important? In some ways I think praying for a particular grace is the grown-up version of praying for fulfilment of desire. By this I mean that praying for the fulfilment of desire is a part of the larger idea of praying for grace. It is essentially the same thing, but the idea of grace becomes crucial when we are praying for something which we do not yet have the capacity to desire. To help explain this, I will illustrate it, at some length, with a very personal experience.

Some time ago, over a period of a few months, I was buffeted by a series of significant emotional challenges. It seemed to me that the only way to get through it all was to face everything head on, at least internally. These challenges included the complete breakdown of an old friendship, as well as cancer, suicide and post-traumatic stress disorder in my extended family. All this coincided with the breaking up of an intimate relationship. It is dealing with one aspect of the last of these which I will use to illustrate the working of grace.

I fell in love with a man whose wife had died of cancer not too long before. Although I didn't realise it at first, he was, at that time, still grieving her death. For the first few months of our relationship he was one step ahead of me in terms of seeming certainty that our relationship had a significant future – and then the grief caught up with him and suddenly he couldn't cope. It became obvious that, unless we accepted a grossly dysfunctional distortion of what had been, it was impossible for us to continue the relationship. We broke up and, after a period of six weeks or so, we began spending time together again, simply as friends. This seemed like the right thing to do because he was not fine. We'd both thought that the termination of the relationship would help end the conflict he was feeling in dealing with grief – although later it seemed to me that he had been simply ignoring it.

I decided that I would give him time to sort himself out before, perhaps, resuming the relationship. After a few more months nothing had changed and I found myself in a very difficult position. Although from one angle it could have been argued that my waiting was a good and generous thing to do, I began to recognise that I was not waiting with freedom, not waiting in freedom. I was treading water, *waiting for the outcome I desired*. And it was eating at me. In the end, after about a month of fairly chronic insomnia, I finally saw the problem. I recognised my interior lack of freedom. I realised that I needed grace. I needed to pray for freedom; I needed to let go of my desired outcome even though (at that point) still allowing for its possibility. I had to let go of the certainty that what I desired was 'right'. I had to pray for the grace of freedom – even as I held the fear that by praying for that grace I was diminishing the possibility of the outcome I desired.

A few weeks after having begun to pray for this grace of interior freedom with respect to this relationship, I reached the point of feeling that I was able to let it go. And indeed it was only as I gained my own freedom that I began to notice that my friend did not appear to be moving towards any real engagement with the things that had got in the way of our relationship. As that came into focus for me, letting go completely became more and more the obvious way to go.

A further factor in the equation was that in the months prior to this relationship I had begun to realise that relationships were a fundamental part of my own self-knowledge, and that creating a community for myself was an important part of life. I had always viewed myself as something of a loner; I had not really desired intimate relationship although I had had a couple of brief relationships in my mid-twenties. The shift in my understanding of the importance of relationship resulted in the desire for relationship, and a few months later this man and I started dating. So in a sense it seemed as though this particular relationship was an answer to my prayer. I have no doubt that this idea also played a role in the difficulty I had in letting go. In retrospect, that crazy time of chaos was extremely useful to me, in that for the first time in my life I allowed my friends to support me in my vulnerability. I have always withdrawn, sorted myself out and then re-engaged. As I became free of my need for this particular relationship to work out, I began to see the substantial shift that had happened within my wider friendship circle. I marked the gaining of my freedom with a small gathering of my close friends, many of whom had not met each other before.

What was crucial to me in the entire process, was my recognition of my lack of freedom and my daring to pray for that freedom, even when it felt incredibly risky. Even when it felt as though praying for that freedom was likely to diminish the probability of the outcome I was desiring. At those times when it felt as though I was risking losing the very thing desired, I prayed for the desire for freedom.

This kind of prayer is one step removed from praying for the thing itself. It is an acknowledgement that I can see what I need, but that I do not yet have the courage to pray directly for that thing. Instead, I pray for the desire to pray for that thing; I pray for the capacity to pray for something which I do not yet have the capacity to desire. In Ignatian terms, this is 'praying for the desire to desire'. (Not an easy concept!)

Going back to the example of my relationship: over time, and with at least daily attention to noticing what I was able to pray for, and praying for the grace that seemed possible, I found that things were beginning to shift. I was aware of gaining freedom, and, once I had that freedom, I was able to see what I needed to do – for myself – was to walk away from the situation. Ultimately, I had the courage to look at my pain, to look at my lack of freedom – and to choose life.

Although I feel awkward about using this very personal example, it is the one which most vividly illustrates the point I am trying to make – about seeking first the desire to desire. Going through this process has had an impact on the way in which I pray. It has certainly had a profound impact on the way in which I view my world. I am beginning to notice my unfreedoms more. Not necessarily on a daily basis, but when they bite a little. It has also made me aware that the insomnia that I have battled with most of my adult life has far more to do with my failing to pay attention to things that are eating at me than with any real physiological deficit.

In *What Doesn't Kill Us: the new psychology of posttraumatic growth*, Stephen Joseph notes that there are three existential themes which emerge from talking with people who have experienced significant personal growth following a traumatic event:

> The first is the recognition that life is uncertain and that things change. This amounts to a tolerance of uncertainty that, in turn, reflects the ability to embrace it as a fundamental tenet of human existence. The second is psychological mindfulness, which reflects self-awareness and an understanding of how one's thoughts, emotions and behaviors are related to each other as well as a flexible attitude toward personal change. The third is acknowledgement of personal agency, which entails a sense of responsibility for the choice one makes in life and an awareness that choices have consequences[31].

This is not to suggest that what I went through amounts to trauma, although the confluence of events provided a substantial emotional challenge. But I would argue that the first point – the recognition that life is uncertain – is important in

31   Stephen Joseph (2011) p.19.

all emotionally challenging circumstances. Inevitably, things will happen in life which will seem like a dead end. A problem may occur which does not seem to have a solution, or at least does not seem to have a desirable solution. A child struggling at school; a serious illness; depression; painful conflict in a family – all of these things are substantial challenges which do not necessarily have obvious solutions. It is in these kind of cases that praying for a grace is enormously helpful.

The importance of being honest with oneself

At the heart of this idea of praying for the grace is a high level of self-reflection and honesty. It requires that I am able to see where I actually am, not where I wish I were. In the scenario above, it would have been so easy to tell myself stories about my generosity in being there for my friend in his time of need. I could have allowed myself to believe that he was doing the work he needed to do and that it was just a matter of time till he dealt with his grief. I was fortunate in that there were some powerful physical signs which indicated all was not well with me – I couldn't sleep after I had seen him, and I found it difficult to eat in his company. In retrospect, as I write this, I am truly astounded that it took me as long as it did to figure out that I needed to find freedom! But in situations of unfreedom, we will do anything we can to perpetuate the myth we do not want to shatter.

Honesty is necessary to cut through the illusion so that we can see the reality – even though it can feel fairly brutal. Most of us are masters at seeing things the way we want to see them instead of seeing them as they are. We project our desires for our reality onto our world and then act as though that is how things are. When life is going well we can get away with that for a long time, but when things crumble it becomes very difficult. This is why the process of taking stock – described in Chapter 1 – is so important. Learning to look at the reality of your current situation from different angles improves the chance that from at least one angle you will glimpse the truth which you are trying to avoid. It is good to practice this kind of honesty when things are going well; it is important to pay attention to the signals the world is giving you.

One example of practising honesty is by using random unsolicited compliments. Some time ago I was having a drink with a friend and we were discussing some responsibility I had taken on. She commented that, like so many of things I do, I would do a good job. I quickly brushed the comment aside and moved on to other things, but her comment stayed with me. For many months I wondered why she would think that. I do not think I do things particularly well, mostly I muddle through, and if there is a lot of other stuff happening I choose the path of least energy expenditure (not something I am particularly proud of!). But it occurred to me, when I was on a six-day retreat some time later, that I am a committed person. By which I mean that if I agree to being involved in something I am committed to it. I do not take things on lightly, and I will see things through even if they get unpleasant. I think this is the reason for the compliment that I was paid. It is not that I am particularly special, it is just that if I agree to something I commit to it and invest in it. I also recognise that not everyone does that to the same extent, and that that quality is attractive.

The point is to pay close attention to the feedback from your world. If you believe that you are great at explaining things, but you are frequently misunderstood then your self-perception may not be accurate. If you think you are a fantastic driver, but have frequent accidents or near misses because of the other idiots on the road, maybe you are not quite as good as you thought. If you struggle with public speaking but are always complimented on your presentations, maybe it's time for you to take the feedback on board.

Praying for the grace that I need relies on my understanding of myself and what is going on in my world. That requires that I am observant of myself and of my world, and, crucially, of the outcomes of the interactions that are going on in my world. The outcomes of my interactions with my world will give me a good idea whether my understanding and interpretation of myself in my world are accurate or not.

The experience of the grace is often not quite what you expect

Oftentimes in directing the Spiritual Exercises, I have found myself listening to a person describing the experience of their prayer. As spiritual director I am, in part, listening for the emergence of the grace associated with that particular Week of the Exercises. As I have mentioned several times now, the grace of the First Week is to recognise that I am a loved sinner. As the conversation progresses, it will become evident that the person themselves has not yet recognised that the experience they are having is in fact the desired grace. He or she will be talking about their sense of amazement at the love of God in the context of a contemplation on their own sinfulness. But frequently they do not put two and two together and recognise that actually this experience that they are describing is exactly the grace that they have been praying for. The lived experience is often not what we imagine it will be.

I find myself still in the process of living into this world of praying for grace and then, quite unexpectedly, noticing that it has emerged. The best example I have of this is my experience of the joy of the Resurrection. The Third Week of the Exercises is praying through Jesus's Passion and Crucifixion, and the Fourth Week is a contemplation of his Resurrection. The grace of the Fourth Week of the Spiritual Exercises is joy with Christ in joy. In mid-2003, I was on an eight-day individually guided retreat at Loyola Hall in England. I found myself praying through the Third and Fourth Weeks, and on the last day I was praying for the grace of joy with the risen Christ in joy. In a very real way, this grace can be an experiential sense of the meaning and power of the Resurrection. I was walking around the field at the back of the grounds talking to God and asking when I would and if I would receive this grace. All of a sudden, as I turned a corner into a carpet of wild flowers, the brown and green of late summer grasses gave way to an explosion of colour – and I understood. The greyscale world gave way to technicolour (I know the world was not actually greyscale before, but that was the sense of it). Before this experience, I would never have thought to describe the transition into the Fourth Week grace in that almost visceral way.

Even now, ten years later, I still have a vivid image in my mind of turning that corner and the emotional surge of joy. That freedom, that joy, has a very particular flavour. Somehow, it contains the pain that has gone before. There is no sense of denial of the pain, and indeed a similar pain may be encountered again, but there is strange shift in that pain from something that is crippling to something that is freeing. I have no real world analogy for that experience. But I have tasted it in enough different contexts now to trust it and to know that something fundamental shifts in me as a result of being present to that pain, praying for the grace and allowing my internal landscape to shift.

In my experience, the emergence of a grace usually has this kind of tangible quality to it. Not necessarily with vivid imagery, but there is often something a little unexpected and a little surprising about the way in which the grace is experienced. Not long ago I was praying for the grace of forgiveness. Forgiving the man I had broken up with, and forgiving myself for my failure to be completely honest with him in the strange and confusing friendship that we moved into after the break up. I had been praying for this grace for some weeks when I spoke on the telephone to my eldest sister. During the conversation I realised that I had forgiven both him and myself. As we were talking I realised that the shift had happened. Interestingly as I write about it now, I am trying to remember exactly what I was grappling with when I was praying for that grace; the memory seems just beyond my reach. But having received the grace, and after the real soul-searching that went with praying for the grace, the detail no longer matters. It is done: I have completed my work.

Sometimes in praying for a particular grace, further insight develops and it becomes clear to you that you actually need to be praying for something a little different. I once had a very negative interaction with someone I knew well. This person blamed me for a great deal of the pain in her life. I had spent substantial time sifting out what part of the blame was truly mine and what was not. When yet another email from her arrived, I found myself praying for the grace to see anything more I might have missed. As the days wore on it became clear that I needed to pray for the grace to walk away in freedom because the continued interaction was not helpful to either of us.

The grace when it emerges may not look the way you expect it to. It may be packaged in surprising ways. Part of the process of praying for the grace is allowing grace to appear as it will. In other words allowing God to be God. Allowing God to give us exactly what we need at that particular time, rather than trying to control the outcome; trying to tell God what to do.

The grace can appear 'undesirable' even though one can see the freedom

It is important to recognise that whilst we may be able to grasp intellectually that a particular grace is a good thing, the emotional desire for it may be lacking. You may be able to see that having the freedom to follow Christ wherever he leads is a good thing, but you may also be too strongly attached to your current situation to feel confident about the possibility of forsaking it. You may want to desire the freedom to be able to move, but are emotionally paralysed when you imagine the reality. In the personal situation I described above, I knew that I wanted the freedom to allow the relationship to be or not be, but that required my being willing to admit that the relationship might really be fully over. It meant letting go of a love. Letting go of love is not something that comes easily. It was the first time I had truly fallen in love; I did not know that I would survive a broken heart. I certainly did not know that in the letting go, I would discover, in a new way, the gift of the friendships I already had.

This way of looking at grace is about bridging the gap between the intellectual and the emotional. One can intellectually recognise the benefit of *seeing* things differently, but actually *choosing* is not quite so simple because one is not yet emotionally in a position to do that. Part of the process, then, of praying for a particular grace is coming to recognise the attachments which are preventing the movement forward. Implicit in this is an awareness of myself in the world. It requires paying attention to the tensions and pains I discover. It requires paying attention to the joy. It requires us to dare to engage with vulnerability, to dare to feel the whole range of emotion. The more I look around, the more I think that the human race is on cusp of a great expansion in life. But we have to choose to grapple with life to get there. The opportunities to engage multiply through therapy, spiritual direction, prayer, meditation and many other activities, but so too, do the distractions multiply – and just as fast. For example, a runner might find that it's not enough to do a half marathon any more; the goal must be increased to a multiday stage race. We seem to be pushing ourselves further and further, not noticing that these challenges are distracting us from the real stuff of life.

Toxic attachments are those which feel as if they are crucial to your identity: they generate the feeling that the loss of this particular job or person or role will mean a loss of the way in which we understand or define ourselves. But a sense of freedom with respect to an attachment does not require that there is no passion or no desire. Attachments in themselves aren't always a problem. We *should* love, and we *should* have preferences. The issue with attachments arises when we make a god of something. I have the most superb spiritual director. She is wise and knowledgeable. She has a good sense of humour and a wealth of compassion. I have known many spiritual directors in my life and none of them quite match up to her. I value her, and celebrate her presence in my life, I know I am the richer for it. But I also know that, if something were to happen which made it impossible to continue in this spiritual direction relationship, God and I will be fine. I am sure I will always view this relationship with great affection and enormous gratitude, but I am equally sure that my relationship with God is not dependent upon its existence. For me, the knowledge that 'God and I will be fine' is a benchmark for my attachments. Others may use a different phrase, for example: 'My sense of self will remain intact'. This is not to say that the loss won't be felt, but simply that the loss doesn't require a complete re-evaluation of my world.

In 2003, I was on a residential course at Loyola Hall, when the possibility of taking a job as a team member there came up. This was a job beyond my wildest dreams. I thought I would be working towards it for the best part of decade, if not longer – the vast majority of spiritual directors are significantly older than the twenty-seven I was at the time. And here it was, almost within my grasp. The night before I had the interview for the job, I sat in the main chapel praying. I remember clearly saying to God: 'I want this job more than anything that I have wanted in my life. I believe that the last five years have been building to this moment. And I also believe that you and I will be fine if it does not work out[32].' There was freedom.

The grace is always accompanied by an increase in real freedom

An increase in real freedom comes precisely because the grace allows us to let go of this particular attachment. Un-

---

[32] I realise now that they would never have interviewed me if they hadn't intended to offer me the job. Given what they knew of me, they would have been almost certain of the outcome. It was almost a fait accompli, but I did not recognise it at that time.

healthy attachments are usually driven by ego or by extrinsic rewards. They are the things – such as money and status – that seem important because they appear to be valued by the world. They can even be 'counter-world' options that we believe contribute to our identity and self-understanding. One of the challenges I faced a number of years ago was the recognition that I am not called to full-time ministry. I had spent four years working in a retreat house and found that, even though the work was enjoyable and rewarding, a part of me was being neglected. Part of my identity had been invested in the idea that I had given up the possibility of a promising career as a research chemist in order to follow Christ. In returning to chemistry research I had to rethink my identity. I was attached to that part of my identity, and part of my journey that year was finding the freedom to let it go.

Attachments come in many different guises and forms. They can also be ideas which provide a safe but extremely limited space for us. We often hear people complaining about trying to get a decent work/life balance. There always seem to be a million and one reasons why finding this balance is so difficult. But the truth of the matter is that for most middle class, educated people there is much more of a choice than we are willing to see. Many of us could have a much more balanced use of time if we were willing to stop actively climbing the career ladder, or if we were willing to take a cut in salary. Of course, the pressures are different if we have a family to support, but nevertheless, we do have much more of a choice than many of us are willing to recognise. It is a sad truth that those who make significant career changes often find the courage to do so only when they are forced to by some external circumstance. I know people who were miserable in their previous jobs and spent countless hours fantasising about having the freedom to make a different choice, but it was only when circumstances such as retrenchment occurred that they found that freedom. Now, of course, it is to be celebrated that such freedom was found. It doesn't always work like that: I also know people who, even on retrenchment, have not been able to think outside their former boxes although they weren't particularly enjoying their job!

The point is simply that most of our attachments are not nearly as immovable as we sometimes think. The issue is not the thing itself, but rather our attitude towards it. If my identity is bound up in my job, then anything that threatens my job will feel like a personal attack, and it would be unthinkable for me to reconsider my job options because that would erode my identity. Similarly if I believe that being in a relationship somehow validates me as a person, then I will be willing to make huge sacrifices to remain in that relationship – simply because in my head any relationship is better than no relationship. My attachment to the concept of relationship causes me to sacrifice parts of myself in order to remain in that relationship. The point here is that the thing itself, the relationship or the job – assuming neither requires me to break the law – is morally neutral. Having a certain job, or being in a certain relationship, is not in itself necessarily evidence of character or lack of it, but my attitude towards that job or that relationship can be healthy or it can be toxic. If I am overly attached to the idea of the thing (and usually the sense of identity that I gain from it) then regardless of whether it is good for me or not, there is a problem.

Because God is God, and God is generous, a person may understand these things in purely psychological terms and still receive grace. Nevertheless, I believe that there is a real benefit in recognising grace as something beyond ourselves. It allows us to really begin to engage with the reality that not everything is within our control.

A grace cannot be willed into being

A grace cannot be willed into being. Perhaps I should begin by explaining what I mean by 'willed into being'. Our particular issue may involve something external, something that is changeable, but we cannot change anything *within* ourselves unless we truly desire it. I think most of us have physical issues we struggle with – a weight problem, lack of exercise, a habit of eating poorly, or something we indulge in a little too much. Unless there is a strong desire or motivating factor to change our behaviour, we find it very difficult to sustain any changes we might feel we ought to make. The will to eat the piece of cheesecake easily overcomes the weak 'I ought not to' when I am offered the cheesecake. Grace in this sense is about overcoming an attachment, something which we know we need to let go of, but something to which at least a part of us is clinging so desperately that we cannot will ourselves into the new mental space. Instead, much like the first steps of the classic 'twelve-step program', we need to admit our lack of freedom in this one area and our lack of power over our own wills. We need to submit this lack of freedom to God, finally, to ask God to release us from our attachment.

The first step is recognising the problem: recognising that our lack of freedom in this particular area is actually toxic. The second step is daring to hold that up before God and to ask for help to become free. The third is choosing to stay in that space of vulnerability before God, or at least returning frequently – mentally, emotionally and spiritually – to that space, until the problem starts to shift. The important distinction between a standard twelve-step program and this movement towards grace is that the 'thing' itself may not necessarily be toxic to our lives. It may, for example, be an unhealthy attitude towards a particular relationship. In this case it is the attitude that is the source of toxicity, not the relationship itself. Ultimately the freedom comes with the willingness for the thing to continue to exist in our lives – or not. When we are attached to something in an unhealthy way, we cannot imagine – nor do we wish to imagine – a life without that thing.

The process thus begins with noticing the toxicity, noticing that something is not right. For me, the alarm bell is usually insomnia, for others it may be frequent headaches, an upset stomach, drinking too much, or picking fights with others. The symptoms will be particular to you and the way in which you deal with things, but if you start paying attention and noticing the areas where your life is not well balanced it will become clear that there is a problem. But noticing the symptoms is just the beginning. If the attachment is very strong, and especially if the object of attachment first presented itself as a blessing or gift, then it may take a while to recognise where the problem actually lies. You may make some false starts, but, sooner or later, something will emerge that is clearly problematic. But a large part of you may still not want to let go. Then it is simply about holding both the desire to keep and the desire to let go before God and asking for the grace of freedom.

In asking for the grace of freedom it is important to understand that you are letting go of controlling the outcome. I have found myself sitting for days with the knowledge that I need to find my freedom with respect to something, but at the same time knowing that I am not willing to give it up. All I do then is hold these conflicting emotions before God and ask that God give me the grace I require. Sooner or later, the willingness to let go emerges and with it usually a sense relief, a sense of sadness and, oddly, a sense of joy. There is a lightness and the world looks just a little different.

Not all graces are about resolving internal problems

So far I've been talking about grace very much in the context of making life choices. Usually in such situations something happens which reveals an attachment. Usually it is because the object of your attachment is somehow threatened. Colleagues are being retrenched, or someone you love is undergoing a major life transition, or your last child is leaving the house. Not all these things will cause problems, but if it seems as though you are about to lose the object of your attachment, the part of you that feels that it will die without that object will start kicking up a fuss and the attachment will be revealed, and the internal 'issue' will emerge.

Nonetheless, sometimes grace is about learning how to deal with life. It is a grace to be able to sit before God with my grief at the death of a relative, to face my sense of loss and perhaps my fears or my lack of desire to go on into this changed world where this person is no longer. Sometimes the circumstances of a death really require processing. If the death is violent in any way – a car accident where reckless driving was involved, a murder, or a suicide – there may be anger to process. The world may look a little different; fears for others in the family may develop. All these things are not pleasant to examine, and it takes time for the real emotion to emerge.

It takes enormous courage to sit with the pain. There can be a fear that the pain may be overwhelming, but there is also a fear of what it would mean if we did allow the immediacy of the pain to pass. It takes courage to allow God to help us to hold this pain and to lead us into life beyond the immediacy of this pain. We do not really want to think that life is possible beyond this pain, because we feel that that would somehow diminish how much we valued the other person or people who might be involved. And somehow we convince ourselves that the strength of our feeling is a measure of the quality of the relationship that has been lost. That idea is nonsense; again it is an ego attachment of sorts. We need to allow God to show us the way through. We need to allow God to be God. We need to dare to allow grace to enter our lives. Grief is not a state that any of us would choose, but how much worse would life be if we protected ourselves from ever experiencing it. Such an isolated life would not be worth much. We experience grief when we move, when relationships come to an end. And so it is useful to recognise the role of grace in helping us navigate our way through the darkness.

The relationship between desire and grace

Praying for the grace does not require that we have a good sense of where it will take us. The process begins with the recognition that all is not well where we are and something needs to change. Over time, as we continue to contemplate our position and we continue to pray for grace to find a way through, a hint of a path may begin to emerge. With more time, the path may become better defined. At first encounter, the path may not look particularly attractive, but we begin to pray for the 'desire to desire' to take that path. And again, over time, we slowly find the desire growing within us and we can begin to take the first steps. Desire, understood in this way, is the trajectory which emerges from grace. The will to take the emergent trajectory follows the desire.

As suggested in the previous chapter, each desire is shaped by different factors in our lives. The capacity to trust in grace and the ability to follow life-giving desire does not usually appear magically when we find ourselves in an intractable situation. To see how it works, we can make an analogy with the way our bodies are able to tolerate extreme stress better and to recover more quickly if we are fit and healthy. It's not that we won't feel the stress, but that we are more resilient if we have taken care of ourselves. So too, if we habitually pay attention to our emotional and spiritual selves, and ensure that we are fit and healthy in this respect, we are far more likely to fare better in times of emotional or spiritual stress.

Conclusion

It is vitally important to remember that this idea of praying for a grace is just one small aspect of grace. The grace of God operates outside the confines of our consciousness. It is unmerited and generous beyond our imaginings. Nonetheless, the experience of praying for a grace and receiving it is enormously powerful. As I have increasingly dared to be honest about my internal landscape, this practice has made me far more aware of my own limitations. And at the same time, I have become much more aware of the power of prayer. Prayer is not primarily about trying to change the external, but rather allowing my internal contours to be moulded to my experience of the world. Through this practice I have caught glimpses of the magnitude of God's grace and have come to realise that it sustains and enriches the world in ways far beyond my understanding.

Pause for a moment and notice what remains with you from this chapter. The material may have been quite challenging.

Who is the God who is with you?

What is the invitation from God?

Do you have an area in your own life where it may be useful to pray for grace?

Chapter 6: Discernment

Let us risk the wildest places, lest we go down
in comfort, and despair
— Mary Oliver

> *Have you ever had the experience of simply being aware of the presence of God?*
>
> *Have you ever been faced with a choice and had a very clear sense of what is right?*

Discernment is the art of noticing the subtle movements of the heart. Discernment helps us to navigate through the turbulent world of conflicting desires.

• •

Many of us find that the different voices that speak in our thoughts pull us in different directions. Discernment is the art of discovering which of those voices lead us deeper into relationship with God and which lead us in a different direction. A way into understanding the art of discernment is learning to distinguish between intrinsic and extrinsic motivations. Learning to distinguish those things which are truly life-giving from those which look attractive but ultimately have little value. In *Daring Greatly*, Brené Brown writes of the distinction between savouring the delicious taste of a piece of chocolate and wolfing down a chocolate bar in an attempt to soothe some other need[33]. One person is capable of both

---

33   Brené Brown (2012) p.146.

of these actions. Discernment is the capacity to distinguish the difference in attitude in myself, and to make choices based on the deeper desires that emerge as I begin to notice what is actually going on.

One of the types of prayer discussed earlier in this book is the examen. This is a prayer of reflection; a prayer of noticing; a prayer of paying attention; a prayer of sifting the wheat from the chaff of our daily lives. As we participate in that process we are using one of the most important spiritual gifts – the gift of discernment. Discernment is the capacity to distinguish between those things that draw us towards God and those things which lead us away from God. I would argue strongly that the greatest gift at the heart of Ignatian spirituality is its teaching on discernment. Discernment gives us a tool to use to distinguish between the really good stuff and the stuff that is simply shiny and attractive. Discernment helps us distinguish between the things that are truly life-giving and the things that seem to offer immediate safety and security. Margaret Silf uses the term 'inner compass' to describe this gift. I like that image – just as a compass unerringly points towards true north, so too we have an inner sense of what will lead us towards God. I realise that is a bold statement to make, and your first response may be one of scepticism. The reason for this is that many of us have learnt to override that inner sense. Sometimes even the Church can teach us to mistrust that inner sense. But if we are truly seeking God, and we take time to stop, to pay attention, to notice, we do find that inner compass. That ability to discern.

You may have a memory from schooldays of being taught about how magnets work. When a piece of iron becomes magnetised, 'domains' of atoms align with one another[34] When that happens, the iron is responsive to the Earth's magnetic field – a compass needle aligns with the Earth's magnetic field to show magnetic north. But magnetism can be disrupted by heating, causing the atoms to lose alignment

---

34   This is, of necessity, a simplified explanation!

with their neighbouring atoms, and the iron will no longer be magnetic. When the metal cools, the atoms will realign and the magnetism will return.

As you have probably realised, I'm using this as a metaphor for noticing how easy it is to lose track of our inner compass when we are fully engaged with all our world has to offer. We live in a world which thrives on overstimulation. Children play on cellphones while watching television, or listen to music while doing their homework. We chat on Facebook while we are trying to work, or surf the net while we chat on the phone. We are so over-stimulated in today's world that things do get jumbled up internally and we can easily lose our ability to discern. But it does not take much to get it back. All that is required is a bit of calm, a gentle quietening, a focusing. And the more we practise that – the more this quiet focusing is a part of our daily routine – the more easily we can find our inner compass when we need it.

A caveat, however. If you are a person who tends towards striving to achieve, or perfection, this is something to incorporate lightly. Attempting to perfect discernment is as much a hindrance as failing to pay attention at all. Discernment is an art that is meant to enhance our experience – not to cripple us with a sense of inadequacy when we get it wrong. The ultimate goal of discernment is not the perfect continuous alignment of the compass needle, it is the capacity to find our inner truth in the midst of engagement with life. Engagement with life will cause perturbation.

How do you discern?

So how do we get in touch with that inner compass? How do we attune ourselves to the sense of God's presence in our daily lives? The most important thing here is that you do not have to learn anything new. You do not have to seek out something different. You simply have to recognise the significance of the experience that you have already had. Take a moment to remember a time when you felt close to God – what was that like, where were you, what was happening for you at that time?

What are some of the feelings you associate with feeling close to God?

Now to shift a little. Take a moment to remember a time when you felt far away from God – what was that like, where were you, what was happening for you at that time?

What are some of the feelings you associate with feeling far away from God?

The question of feeling close to God or far away from God may seem a little abstract. If so, start with a different couplet: What are the feelings you associate with being fully alive? What are the feelings you associate with being constrained or diminished in your being? Or use some other pair of questions which put you in touch with the experience of tasting the essence of your being.

If you have a memory of occasions which fall into each of those two categories, you have the two crucial touchstone experiences for discernment. In the *Exercises*, Ignatius speaks of movements of spirits. It is clear that he expects any healthy Christian person to experience both movements of good spirits and movements of bad spirits. Note here that 'spirits' is a general term applied to pretty much anything that stirs us – nothing like the cartoon caricature of an angel sitting on one shoulder and a demon on the other. His phrase 'movements of spirits' refers to the interactions of feelings, thoughts, and impulses of attraction and recoil which occur spontaneously in consciousness. In other words anything that stirs us internally, no matter what its origin. Ignatius expects a continual motion of some kind to exist. He even goes so far as to say that if the spiritual director is not perceiving any movements of spirits in the one making the Exercises then the exercitant is to be closely questioned as what they are doing[35].

For Ignatius, a lack of movement of spirits is not a sign of spiritual maturity, it is a sign of disengagement. If you think about this in terms of desire it makes perfect sense. Not a day goes by when there is not some shift in desire. Our response to any desire, no matter how large or how small, has the capacity to move us towards God or away from God. Those movements are happening daily, hourly, whether we choose to be aware of the effect or not. Our desires can lead us in different directions. Our desires can lead us towards God or away from God. Our desires can lead us into deeper relationship with others or out of those relationships. Our desires can lead us into a more authentic, more integrated sense of self, or they can lead to greater fragmentation. And oftentimes the trajectory of the desire is entirely subjective. For one person a particular desire may lead Godward, whilst for someone else that same desire can lead in the opposite direction.

Consolation and desolation

Ignatius uses the terms 'consolation' and 'desolation' to describe these two touchstones. The word consolation is not used in the usual English way. Consolation, in this context, is both an experience of the presence of God and those movements which lead us towards God. Desolation, likewise, is not used in the usual English sense. Desolation is the experience of feeling separated from God and those movements which lead us away from God. Consolation is not necessarily always a 'good' feeling. It is possible to be in the midst of intense pain and still feel close to God. This is still consolation. Likewise, it is possible to feel contented and yet be moving away from God. This is still desolation. Consolation and desolation primarily describe our orientation with respect to

---

35   George Ganss (1992) [6].

God rather than the feeling of being consoled or desolate in the way that we would usually understand those words.

There are two exercises above which ask about the feelings you associate with feeling close to, or far from God. They have a simple purpose: to let you see how discernment operates in your own life. I could give a summary of all of Ignatius' rules for discernment of spirits, but it is far more useful, and far more appropriate to the spirit of the *Exercises*, to give you a tool to use.

> *Ask yourself whether the desire that you are examining – whatever it may be – increases the kinds of feelings that your associate with consolation, or not? Not simply at the surface level, but all the way down.*
>
> *Ask yourself questions such as these:*
> *Does this lead me to a greater sense of communion with God?*
> *Does this lead me to a greater sense of being more fully myself?*
> *Is this leading me towards authenticity or away from it?*
> *Does this lead me into greater generosity, or do I find myself defending what is mine?*

For some decisions, we have to dig our way through the surface turmoil to access the deeper reality. One of the best ways to do that is to talk to God about the surface turmoil. Once you have given the fears a voice and a seat in the gallery, they will often let you glimpse the real action, albeit perhaps only momentarily. The surface turmoil must be faced, but make sure it does not drown out the gentle whispering down below.

As I mentioned in Chapter 4, for most of us who are actively seeking God, discernment is not between the good and the bad. It is between the good and the better. So asking the question 'Is this right or wrong?' is not all that helpful. It far more useful to ask questions such as 'What am I really desiring here?' 'What is God desiring?' 'Where do I find myself most fully alive?' 'How is God looking at me as I contemplate making this choice?'

If we are to become mature Christians we need to learn the art of discernment. Too many of us abdicate responsibility in this respect. We want to be told what is good for us to do. We want a simple set of rules to follow. Whilst that may be a good recipe for a quiet life (although I am not sure about that!) we will find it more difficult to discover our heart's desire; we will find it harder to see our true calling; we may not find personal vocation that way. It is only by wrestling with the gamut of unruly emotions and risking getting it horribly wrong that we will find the Source of Life.

In the introduction to this book, I commented that Ignatian spirituality is a spirituality which is accessible to everyone. It is a spirituality for those of us who live ordinary lives. Its focus on finding God in all things means, as I've said, that we can find God in all the days – even in the midst of the crazy chaotic days, and despite the dead boring days – which comprise our lives. Ignatian spirituality also gives us a way to sift our desires. It is not a spirituality of withdrawal or denial. It is a spirituality of engagement. It allows us to take our desires seriously, and to engage with them in prayer.

There is a saying that ships in harbour are safe, but that is not what ships are built for. We have a choice, we can sit in the safe harbour of the rules that we have been taught, or we can choose to risk setting sail, finding out what it means to love, what it means to truly engage with life.

Testing discernment

There are two key testing grounds for any desire. Both require attention and both require discernment. The first is prayer: What happens when I bring this desire into prayer? Am I able to pray honestly about it? I don't think this question is as clear cut as it may seem at first glance. When I bring this thing into prayer am I willing to allow God to be God? Am I willing to explore my motivations? When I was twenty, halfway through my Bachelor of Science degree, I decided that I wanted to study medicine. For eighteen months I pursued that dream, until, through a slightly bizarre set of circumstances, I did not get accepted into any medical school. About a year later as I was thinking back on what had happened, I realised that my principal motivation had not actually been to become a doctor. My principal motivation had been to avoid thinking what I should do with my life. During the course of my BSc, I had discovered that I was pretty good at learning things. Medicine guaranteed me six years of learning stuff, and not having to think about where my life was going. Although I was bitterly disappointed at the time, I am now deeply grateful at the way things turned out.

The point here is simply that I would have saved myself a lot of confusion and heartache if I had known how to pray in a way that allowed reflection and conversation with God about the things I was considering. At the time I didn't really know how to talk to God about the stuff of my life. Now, when I am considering a particular desire, I find I learn a lot about the desire itself, and about my relationship to it, by taking time to consider how I deal with that desire in prayer. A lack of honesty in my prayer can indicate two different things: a knowledge that this thing is really not going to be particularly good for me, and I hope God will not notice; or a great desire for this particular thing and a fear that I will not get it. It is worth noting again that honesty in prayer is the only starting condition that God requires.

The second key arena for discernment is life itself. We do not know that we have made a good discernment until we have tried it out in the real world. This is important in two different ways. Firstly, any discernment must be tested. What does this mean? Regardless of my own certainty that this is the right thing, I need to see what happens in the real world. If I have discerned that a particular path is the right one, and doors open to me along the same avenue, then it is likely that my discernment has been good. However, if I find closed doors, then it is probably a good idea to revisit the initial discernment: am I sure that my motivation is what I'm telling myself it is? It is also possible that the idea is good but the timing is not yet quite right. Secondly, does this, in fact, lead me in a good direction? If I have discerned well and doors open, my task of discernment is not yet over. I must ascertain whether this is actually leading me into deeper relationship with God, into deeper relationship with others, and into a greater sense of personal integrity and authenticity. This is only revealed with time. If it does lead towards God, then continue, but if it does not, you may need to look again, discern again, choose again.

Just to be clear: I do not think that every good choice necessarily leads to deeper relationship with God, deeper relationship with others and a greater sense of personal integrity and authenticity. However, at least one of those things should be true. And if one of those things is true, it is unlikely to be so at the cost of the other two. Another way of looking at this is to examine the value of the choice in terms of its meaning or purpose. A choice that truly leads to life will have some meaning, some sense of purpose, even if it simply seems to be drawing you into a deeper connection with life. A spirituality which takes desire seriously requires us to trust that the pursuit of desire is the entry into deepening relationship with God, and to know that not all desires are equal. So discernment is vital.

Again I just want to remind you that the heart of discernment is your own experience of God. At the heart of Roman Catholic doctrine is a key phrase 'in good conscience'. Acting in good conscience requires that we inform ourselves of the Church's teaching. But ultimately, when we have made choices, we need to be able to stand before God and defend those choices. Defend them in terms of what we have been told is right, but not only that: defend them also because we have sat with the choice in prayer and have discovered a sense that it is indeed the right choice at that time.

Living in South Africa with the history of the justification of apartheid by the Dutch Reformed Church clearly illustrates the problem of simply bowing to authority. Rather, we need to sit with our choices in prayer and allow the Holy Spirit to probe our honesty and integrity. There will be times where it may be necessary, for the sake of conscience, to take a path which is not officially sanctioned. (I would strongly recommend a conversation with a good spiritual director if you find yourself in this position.) As I keep stressing, for the most part the choices we make are not only between right and wrong, but rather between the good and the better. It is important that we take cognisance of the rules and laws of the Church and the State, but ultimately, we must stand before God in good conscience – and discernment allows us a mechanism by which to do this.

Some pointers

There are several useful guidelines which can help you as you start to use discernment:

1. For those who are seeking greater depth of relationship with God, the action of the good spirit can be likened to water dropping into a sponge – it is frequently quiet, gentle and sweet – whilst the action of the bad spirit is more like water splashing onto a stone – there is a jarring, jangling feel to it. The action of the good spirit tends to be gently encouraging, whilst the action of the bad spirit is frequently characterised by phrases which include the words 'ought' and 'should'. If you have made it this far into this book but you're reading it because you feel you 'should', then that action – motivated by guilt – is probably not initiated by the good spirit. If you feel the need to do something and recognise that a sense of guilt is your motivation – take a look at that. It is important information. Spend some time in prayer before you act.

2. It is possible to be tempted under the guise of good. That is to say, not all things which appear to be 'good'

or purposeful or meaningful will lead us towards God. This particular point is premised on the notion that we are able to discern adequately between that which is good and that which is not good. An example of this kind of discernment from the life of Ignatius is his temptation to prayer, mentioned in the Introduction. His principal task at the time was to study, but he found himself drawn into prayer for hours on end. His studies suffered, as did his health, since he was depriving himself of sleep. The desire to pray looks like a good desire, but it led Ignatius away from the very thing he was supposed to be doing. Many of us get trapped by similar things – for some people the temptation is to respond to any opportunity to 'do good' – and as a result their most valued relationships often get neglected. For some the temptation is to spend endless hours in prayer; as a result action is ignored. Even praying can be an escape mechanism – for instance from study, if you are a student. Your particular inclination is important; know where you get caught up. But do not worry about it; just talk to God about it – and in the future make sure you notice those times when you go down a similar route.

3. You are unlikely to be able to determine whether a particular good desire will lead you into deeper relationship with God or not until at least some time has been spent in discernment. I do not think discernment is possible without prayer. This is because the touchstone that we use for discernment is encounter with God, and if we bring encounter with God to the forefront of our minds we are engaged in some form of prayer. In my own experience, I am frequently surprised by which desires in fact lead me into deeper relationship with God and which do not. As an example, my choice to leave Loyola Hall and return to chemistry has been enormously fruitful both in terms of my relationship with God and in terms

119

of my ministry, but to the outsider it could have appeared that I was choosing the less 'Godward' option. Of course this also varies from person to person. The very things I desire and pursue which lead me into deeper relationship with God may prove quite damaging for a different person making the same choice. Or indeed for me, at some other time.

It is important to remember that discernment is a way of life rather than simply a skill that we master. Discernment is an ongoing art. Ignatius expects that anyone engaging properly in relationship with God will be stirred by different desires, and they will sometimes choose correctly and sometimes not. Ignatius is deeply suspicious of the impassive person. We are all on a dynamic developing journey. We cannot possibly hope to choose correctly all the time. The key is to keep noticing. You may notice that you are no longer on the path that you thought you were on and you seem to have turned away from God at some point. But do not beat yourself up or get stressed. Simply turn back to God.

Gerry O'Mahoney SJ, one of my colleagues at Loyola Hall, gives a heartening analogy: Imagine that the desired outcome is to walk with your face towards the sun. The sun represents God in the analogy. Sometimes things will happen and you get distracted by the busyness of life and suddenly you notice that you are looking down at your own shadow. This means that somehow you have got yourself turned around and are now facing directly away from the sun. At that point, you do not have to walk back along the path you have just taken, retracing your steps until you reach the point where you began to steer off course. No, all you have to do to see the sun again is to turn through a hundred and eighty degrees and continue on your journey.

Once you have found your orientation again, and have reconnected with God, it is useful to reflect on the trajectory of your journey. It is useful to understand what it was that caught your attention and led you astray. Did you become overconfident in your ability to steer the course yourself? Were you distracted by what other people were doing? Did you put more faith in the advice of others than in your own sense of what was right for you? The more you practise discernment, the more confidence you will have in your ability to discern. You will begin to notice the subtle difference between what is actually real and what you were just hoping was true.

Discernment is not a big battle between opposing desires. Desire is fuelled by attention. Pay attention to those desires that seem to be leading Godward and simply leave aside those which do not. As Ignatius puts it: 'The good that they might be followed and the bad that they might be left aside...' If you find yourself consumed by something which you have discerned is not leading you Godward, trying to fight it can often just add fuel to the fire. Find something to distract yourself. As a ridiculously trivial example, there have been two occasions in my life when I have been a little overweight, both precipitated by fairly intense loneliness. On both occasions when I tried to diet to lose weight I found the continual thinking about food and calorie counting resulted in my gaining more weight. When I let the issue go and simply got on with living, along with finding emotional support, my weight dropped back down without any real effort on my part. My desire for emotional support, once attended to, took care of the food consumption, but focusing on the food meant that I just ate more. If a desire is genuinely a desire, and not a compulsion, Ignatius' strategy will normally work very effectively. (But please note that if you do uncover a compulsion or two along the way, you would probably do well to find some help.)

One of the most effective aids to good discernment is talking about the desire. The first place for that conversation is prayer; the second may well be something like spiritual direction. There is nothing like exposing our desires to the light of day to help us figure out the trajectory of the desire. Our inability or unwillingness to articulate a desire is not necessarily a sign that it should be left alone: it may simply mean that the time is not yet right for this particular thing to come to fruition. Again, the key is simply noticing and paying attention. If you do choose to articulate your desires to another person, be very selective about the person you choose to help you discern. Ideally it should be a person who is not personally invested in what you choose, but has your best interests in mind. You need to be careful though: family members and close friends may well have your best interests in mind, but they may not be able to get past their own ideas of what is best for you. Ignatius writes that the spiritual director 'ought not lean or incline in one direction or the other, but rather be like the pointer of a scale in equilibrium'. It is often very difficult for those who are somehow immersed in our lives to attain that level of freedom with respect to a particular desire.

It is important to go into prayer with an open mind and heart. Do not presume to know the answer before you pray. Let God be God! Allow God to show you what God wants you to see. Trust that God will not let you go astray. God will provide hints, clues and signs about the way forward. If you are actively seeking God you will be able to recognise at least some of these. God is always actively trying to communicate with us. But if we do not really want to hear what God is saying then we are fully capable of justifying our self-focused actions. Once again, the importance of the priority of honesty with ourselves emerges. Discernment requires that we pay attention not only to our desires, but also to the deepest motivation we are able to access. We may not always be able to access the underlying motivations, but we can be sure that we will not find them if we are not looking for them! It takes practice to be able to sift through the different interior levels, to know how it feels when we have found the real reason.

In 2003 I took a spiritual direction course at Loyola Hall. On the first evening Rob Marsh SJ began by leading us through a very simple but powerful prayer exercise. We began by getting a sense of where God was, then he asked 'Why are you here?' and paused for few minutes. Then he said 'No. Why are you *really* here?', again pausing for a few minutes. Finally, he said 'Why does God think you are here?' It was a powerful exercise, and my answers to the three questions were different each time. I continue to use this periodically in my own prayer when I am trying to discern whether a particular choice is worth pursuing or not. It gives me access to more than my initial response. More often than not, my initial sense of whether to pursue something or not is upheld. But I have been surprised by the need to change my mind often enough to know that I need to keep an open mind – and to allow God to be God.

Conclusion

Discernment is far more about getting a feel for something; noticing a slight inclination in one direction. There are no guarantees and little certainty. It frequently takes a while longer than is comfortable. There may well be a fair bit of trial and error involved. Remember that the focus is deepening relationship with God, not perfecting discernment. I do not think it is possible to perfect discernment anyway, but it is very easy to start focusing on that. It is a great temptation to blame yourself because you discernment was off. It is at that point that you really are going wrong – when you notice you are heading in a direction which does not seem to be leading towards God. Stop, notice where God is, and continue in that direction. God is always there, it is just that we periodically lose sight of God.

What are the things that lead you into deeper relationship with God?

What are the things that get in the way of that?

What helps you to pay attention to the still, small voice?

What things distract you from that?

Who are the people who support your search for God?

Who are the people who get in the way of that?

Take a moment to give thanks to God for the things that are supporting.

Chapter 7: Indifference

Navigation by destination has to give way to something more subtle: finding our way by finding God's way
— *Rob Marsh SJ*

So far we have tracked our way through desire and discernment. Suggestions have been made, but in the end we are still fundamentally limited by the way in which we view our world. This chapter is essentially about the recognition that the real call in our lives is to allow God to lead us through the extraordinary experience of being human.

Have you ever had the experience of thinking something was going to be wonderful and it turned out not to be so, or that something was going to be a bit gruelling but it turned out to be a blessing? Those kinds of experiences remind us of our limitations. Learning to allow God to be God is a lifelong task.

••

What is indifference?

It is perhaps worth spending a little time on a fundamental theme of Ignatian spirituality – that of indifference. It is important to begin by noting that the common English usage of the word 'indifference', which is somewhat akin to 'I don't care', is not what is intended by the word in this context. Rather it gives us a way to focus our attention on desire that truly leads us into deeper relationship with God.

I spent about a year going to a life coach. In the beginning it was useful. I had chosen to do this because I had been struggling to find a spiritual director. As the year progressed I found myself increasingly frustrated by the 'coaching' process because my coach kept encouraging me to make goals such as the amount of money I wanted to save, or the number of papers I wanted to have written within particular time frames. Looking back I realise that the reason I found this frustrating was that the desires she was encouraging me to name, pursue and realise were all hedonic desires. They may have been of incidental benefit to my community, but essentially they were things that I had identified as achievements that would allow me to feel good about myself or gain some extrinsic reward. I stopped going to see her because it felt as if I was not being encouraged to celebrate life as it was for me at that moment. As I look at it now, I recognise that she was encouraging me to pursue success, but very little emphasis was placed on meaning and being. The desires which she naturally focused on were hedonic desires, where I had long been practising focusing on eudaemonic desires. (This is not to suggest that I do not have hedonic desires, but rather that I find emphasising eudaemonic desires far more rewarding in the long run.)

So far in this book we have encountered fragments of the Principle and Foundation from *The Spiritual Exercises*, but it is useful in the exploration of the idea of indifference to look at Ignatius' whole paragraph. In his book, this paragraph appears just after the purpose of the *Exercises* is explained. It is the foundation upon which the *Exercises* is built. It gives a concise summary of Ignatius' worldview.

Principle and Foundation

Pause here for a moment. Spend some time reading over the section below, noticing what draws you, and what is less appealing.

Talk to God a little about those things.

126

Human beings are created to praise, reverence, and serve God our Lord, and by means of doing this to save their souls.

The other things on the face of the earth are created for the human beings, to help them in the pursuit of the end for which they are created.

From this it follows that we ought to use these things to the extent that they help us toward our end, and free ourselves from them to the extent that they hinder us from it.

To attain this it is necessary to make ourselves indifferent to all created things, in regard to everything which is left to our free will and is not forbidden. Consequently, on our own part we ought not to seek health rather than sickness, wealth rather than poverty, honor rather than dishonor, a long life rather than a short one, and so on in all other matters.

Rather, we ought to desire and choose only that which is more conducive to the end for which we are created[36].

At first glance the phrase 'we ought not to seek health rather than sickness, wealth rather than poverty, honor rather than dishonor, a long life rather than a short one, and so on in all other matters' is vaguely reminiscent of wedding vows: For better or for worse; for richer, for poorer; in sickness and in health... We can get behind that idea when it comes to promising ourselves to the one we love. Notice here though, that Ignatius is talking about freeing ourselves from the need to pursue health, wealth, honour, and all similar things, precisely to free ourselves to choose the way that God is leading. It seems a little crazy – especially not seeking health – and is

---

36   George Ganss (1992) [23].

certainly quite counter-cultural, but it is important to recognise that this idea of being indifferent to things is precisely
to provide us with the freedom we need to focus on the essential.

For Ignatius the essential thing is the salvation of our souls.
David Fleming SJ in his contemporary reading of the *Exercises*[37] expresses it this way: 'The goal of our life is to live with
God forever.' I certainly find the substitution of relationship
with God a lot easier to grasp than the salvation of my soul.
This, I believe, is closely related to finding meaning and purpose in life. It is not quite the same thing, but the idea of indifference can probably be more easily understood if we look
at the importance of finding meaning and purpose – which
seems a little more tangible than relationship with God. As
we will see, 'meaning and purpose' does not fully hold the
idea of indifference, but at least it gives us a way in.

There is a great deal of research which shows that, once you
are past a certain threshold income, having money does not
correlate with happiness. And yet so many of us still actively
pursue financial reward as if it were the key to happiness. In
the same way, we seek status and purchase all sorts of things
to gain social acceptability. What Ignatius is pointing out
here is that we need to be very careful about pursuing 'the
good life'. Not because there is anything inherently wrong
in having money or status, but rather because it is hard to
focus on what is really important when we have a fixed idea
of what happiness or contentment will look like. We need to
be free of a desire for wealth, in order to be able to choose
the lower-paying job which has far greater meaning for us.
In order to be free to choose a path of meaning, a path of
high intrinsic value, we need to be free of the expectations of
extrinsic appearance.

If this focus on eudaemonic desire is not immediately apparent from the Principle and Foundation, we see it emerge

---

37   David Fleming (1996) [23].

again more explicitly in an exercise called the Kingdom exercise. The Kingdom exercise is introduced in the *Exercises* at the beginning of the Second Week – once we know that we are loved sinners. In the Kingdom exercise we are invited, in our loved brokenness, to be disciples: companions of Jesus. In this exercise, Ignatius asks that we imagine ourselves standing before a great earthly leader: someone who is a good person, worthy of respect, who asks us to join in a campaign towards the achievement of a substantial and meaningful project. He asks that we imagine our response to that call. Then he takes it a step further and asks that we imagine, now, standing before Christ, being asked to participate in the project of making the world a more compassionate, more loving, more forgiving place. How much more worthy is Christ of our allegiance than the great human leader. In so doing, Ignatius sets the stage for a life of intrinsic value.

Indifference begins, then, with the capacity to let go of our need to specify the external decoration (where we need to live, how much money we need to have, the level of status and recognition that we want) in order to allow the eudaemonic desire to truly blossom. This is why indifference does not mean a lack of passion. We can be as passionate as we like about our search for meaning, our search for purpose, our search for God – and we should stoke that passion. But we need to develop our capacity to allow God to be God and to show us the best way that we can live that passion. We need to develop freedom with respect to the detail of what that living will look like.

It is important to note at this juncture, that it is unlikely that a genuine search for meaning will be destructive for those around you. The blossoming of a eudaemonic desire will normally be accompanied by a growth in compassion and empathy.

Ignatian indifference opens the space to let God be God. It reminds us that however much we may think we know what is good for us, we are not able to see the full picture. It also allows for the reality of our living in a broken world, in which circumstances often require the cooperation of people who may be focusing on shoring up their own egos rather than on the greater glory of God.

This idea of indifference is totally counter-cultural in an era which is so image-conscious. Driving the right car, having the right cellphone, being seen at the right places is so much a part of our world today. We cannot put off seeking meaning until we have more time, or have accumulated enough to have the luxury of focusing on the 'important stuff'. This is something that we have to begin to practise now. We cannot be sure that we will in fact have the time to focus on meaning later on; and importantly, what we choose to focus on today will shape the desires we have tomorrow. If we put off focusing on meaning until we 'have enough' we will never get there.

The powerful idea at the heart of Ignatian indifference is that if we focus on the essential desire – the desire for God – this itself brings a sense of purpose and meaning to life. Within this context, it is possible to choose anything. The extrinsic rewards no longer have the same pull, so we are able to make the choice to live simply. We are able to make the choice to follow God where God leads.

Taking it further

For many years, I understood indifference primarily in terms of making life choices. My experience of indifference was very much tied in with times of making choices: for example the experience in the chapel the night before my job interview at Loyola Hall, described in Chapter 5. But I have also experienced the need for indifference in the context of interpersonal relationships. Following the breakdown of the love relationship described in the same chapter, I found myself still entangled in its emotional baggage. At a certain point

I had to make a decision about whether to attend a friend's wedding in the UK. The day that I really had to choose whether to go or not, I realised just how bound I was by residual emotional baggage. I realised that the principal reason that I wanted to go to the UK was to distract myself from the internal emotional turmoil.

At that point I realised the extent of my lack of internal freedom. I was out on a walk that I take quite frequently at lunch time. The route leads into a small nature reserve which has a labyrinth. I walked the labyrinth and set before God my own lack of freedom. The difficulty at the heart of the experience was that to gain freedom I had to let go of my hope that the relationship would be restored. The challenge was that I wanted the freedom but I did not want to let go of the hope. So I sat in the centre of the labyrinth for some time. I sat with my pain, my sense of loss, and my own lack of freedom. I sat with my desire for the relationship to be restored. I am a person with quite a strong will, and if I set my mind on a particular goal I can normally find my way there, but in this circumstance I could not will myself to freedom. I sat with my desire for freedom and held my confusion, my pain and my fear before God. Asking that God would help me to find the interior freedom I needed to move forward. I walked back to my office and was surprised to find, that even by the time I drove home a few hours later, I had the beginnings of an inkling of recovering that interior freedom – that Ignatian indifference.

I think what I found surprising in the process was my recognition of the destructive force of the lack of freedom in my life: recognising what needed to be done, and yet having no desire to act. When I held all of these things together in prayer, I discovered God's incredible grace. The desire to move away began to grow, the interior freedom took root and the healing could begin. But it only happened because I was willing to sit with my pain in prayer and to trust that God would show me a way through in God's good time.

And further still

It is worth repeating here the quotation from Rob Marsh SJ that begins the chapter. 'Navigation by destination has to give way to something more subtle: finding our way by finding God's way.' When we cling to our own ideas of how things should be, or where we want to end up, it is easy to lose sight of relationship with God. We do not mean to, but somehow, when we get the bit between our teeth and run off in pursuit of a particular end, we can miss the gentle invitation to encounter God. We can become so focused on the destination that we forget that it is the journey that is really the stuff of life.

Once we have found our sense of purpose – a way of living a robust and fruitful eudaemonic life – it can be tempting to presume that we have arrived. Indifference requires that we continue to be aware that there is no 'arrival' point. There are places where we can allow ourselves to take root, to be fruitful, to engage fully, but even these places may not be permanent. As our lives evolve, there may be a call to a new place. The reminder that we will find the best way through when we seek God's way is crucial. It is far too easy to lose sight of our real goal – deepening relationship with God – in our attempts to make a contribution to the Kingdom. We quickly over-identify with the roles we have found ourselves called into. We can get distracted by the significance of the contribution we are able to make. It is not that such things are not valuable and important, it is just that we have to continually make the choice for the pearl of great price. It is not a once-off choice. It is a choice that will return over and over again. It is when we relax into the certainty that we have the pearl firmly in our grasp that we run into trouble. Indifference is the invitation to hold the pearl we have so lightly that we can trade it in for something more fitting as we develop and grow.

In my own life this is perhaps best illustrated by the time I spent at Loyola Hall. I will never forget the overwhelming sense of relief I felt in walking through the gates for the first time, followed by the growing affirmation of my gift as spiritual director and finally getting the job there. I had a profound sense of being exactly where I needed to be and yet at the same time I had the interior freedom to sit with it lightly (this took noticing my lack of freedom a few months into actually doing the job, some prayer and some grace!). Three and a half years later I found myself making the choice that would have been unthinkable to me in the early months at Loyola Hall as I basked in the consolation of the confirmation of my discernment. I found myself freely choosing to return to chemistry. I still find that choice surprising and I have written elsewhere in this book about this choice, but the capacity to allow God to call me back to a path I thought I had left behind, is the kind of navigation of which Rob Marsh speaks. It is a willingness to follow precisely where God seems to be leading. I should add that this capacity ebbs and flows in me. It is not a constant, but even though I feel now that I am in the right place, doing the right thing at the right time in the right way, I am aware that this too may pass. There may come a time when I find myself needing to take a different tack in some way.

Indifference then is the capacity to invest fully in where we are whilst sitting lightly to it. This is possible only because we do not have to wait for the elusive 'one day' to encounter God, or indeed to become fully ourselves. We have access to that right now, but we begin to glimpse it only when we allow God to be God. We must allow for the possibility that God may call us from the path that has been so fruitful thus far. This is not to say that we need to second guess ourselves all the time as that can really get in the way of living, but rather that we allow for possibility that God may have a different idea.

In summary

Returning to the example of the night before my interview for the job at Loyola Hall: Ignatian indifference is not an easy concept; it is the capacity to hold the desire for something along with a sense of freedom with respect to that thing. Of course I would have been disappointed if I hadn't got the job, but I was willing to let God be God in the process. On that night, I really was able to see that I might not get the job, but I also knew that if that happened it wouldn't have anything to do with my giftedness as a spiritual director, or my sense of call to that ministry. In other words, that my failure to get the job would not have been a personal failure.

I believe that the experience of that kind of indifference or freedom is a grace. It is not a state we can will ourselves into, and it is usually temporary. Nonetheless it is vitally important because it allows for a healthy separation between success in a particular venture and relationship with God. Even if we consciously avoid the prosperity gospel messages which suggest that material wealth is indicative of a right relationship with God, it is easy to fall for the more subtle message that success is somehow predicated upon or linked to the quality of our relationship with God. So failure becomes very difficult, because not only do we have to deal with the reality of the failure itself, but at the same time it can have a major impact on the very place we would turn to for solace – prayer. It is precisely in this place that we discover the power of indifference. Indifference allows for the separation of our success from our image of ourselves. It is a place of real humility, of knowing our own giftedness and of being able to see our rejection or failure in perspective. Indifference opens up a space where we can explore failure – with God, in prayer.

Have you ever had this kind of freedom – a driving passion coupled with a knowledge that you could walk away?

Is your relationship with God sufficiently robust for this to be the deciding factor in your choices?

How does this kind of indifference work in the light of your relationships and responsibilities?

Do you sense an invitation to pray for indifference in any specific area of your life?

Take some time to talk to God about these things.

Chapter 8: Making Decisions

What are you going to do with your one wild and precious life?
— Mary Oliver

Pause for a moment and consider your life.

What tools have you used in the past to help you make the big decisions?

What has influenced things like your career path, your choice of life partner, where you live?

Did you make these choices consciously, or did you stumble into them?

What are the things that you do take into consideration when you make decisions?

The baggage

Any life decision comes with baggage. In making these decisions we frequently need to take other people into consideration. The financial viability of our choices also has an impact. The material in this chapter does not in any way negate the importance of these kinds of issues. The purpose of this chapter is not to provide pointers on how to deal with these things, because they vary in importance for different people and at different times. The purpose of this chapter is to look at the ways in which we can begin to take the will of God into consideration when we make decisions. This is as applicable to those who have specific responsibilities as it is to those who are freer to make choices based simply on their own desires.

We have already looked a fair bit at our own desires, and what influences them. In this chapter we look at the desire to seek the will of God.

If we are genuinely seeking God, it is important to consider what we desire when making important life decisions. But this on its own is not sufficient. We also need to consider what God may desire for us. Part of the chapter on discernment (Chapter 6) aims to help us notice what God seems to be doing, and what God may be desiring. It is important to consider what God may desire. Many of us, when faced with important life decisions tend to err on one side or the other: we either are completely focused on what we ourselves want, or we are completely focused on figuring out what God wants. Either way we end up in a little bit of trouble. It has often been said that God's desire for us is the same as our own deepest desire. We severely limit ourselves, therefore, if we attempt to make good decisions without taking heed first of our own desires, and then taking those desires into prayer, in order to discern what God seems to be desiring for us. We say we are trying to make a good decision, but we are failing to pay attention to half the information.

A couple of pitfalls

A problem with focusing too much on what God wants is that the messages are sometimes not packaged in ways we expect and we miss them. In some ways we can be like the man in the flood. As the waters start to rise, the man prays to ask God to save him, and being a man of good faith he believes that God has heard his prayer and will respond to it. Not long after, someone paddles by in a row boat and encourages him to get on board, to which he responds: 'No; God will save me.' The water rises further and he climbs to the upper story. Someone goes by in a motor boat and says: 'Come on, we will rescue you,' to which the man again responds: 'No; God will save me.' The water rises further still; he is sitting on his roof, when someone flies over in a helicopter. They send down a ladder and encourage him to climb on, to which he says: 'No, no; God will save me.' The man drowns, and when he gets to heaven he says to God: 'I prayed; why did you not answer me?' To which God responds: 'I sent you a rowboat, and a motorboat, *and* a helicopter. What were you waiting for?'

So if we expect to hear a James Earl Jones type baritone in our heads, we are probably going to be waiting a long time. Think back to the rules for discernment of spirits: the action of the good spirit is quiet, gentle and sweet, like water dropping into a sponge. This means that if we are already living a life congruent with seeking God, we are unlikely to receive a message that is going to stop us in our tracks just to convince us that we are headed in the right direction. It does not happen that way. The powerful conversion stories that you hear are always from people who were headed down a quite different path. For those who are already seeking God and who are already on the right track, communication from God is more akin to a gentle nudging and a whiff of affirmation.

The problem with focusing too much on what we want is that most of us do not really know ourselves all that well. We are not fully aware of what really drives us, and that lack of awareness can take us into all sorts of trouble. We make choices based on unconscious drives, and these forces may not necessarily lead us into a deeper, more authentic sense of self. A few years ago, the book *The Secret* was all the rage – its basic premise was that we create our own reality, and that, if you just think in the right way, you can achieve everything you want to. The presumption being that achieving all these things will make you happy. The truth is that we only have to look at those who have achieved enormous success and yet remain discontented to understand that success is not enough to give us inner peace and joy. This comes back to understanding the difference between intrinsic and extrinsic motivations and hedonic and eudaemonic desires.

Here again we encounter the need to be honest with ourselves – or as honest as we are able to be.

How do we begin?

So how do we do this? How do we discover our own desires, and how do we discover God's desires for us? For starters, as implied in Chapter 6, we cannot expect to recognise the movement of the good spirit when we need to make a major life decision if we have not already trained ourselves in the art of discernment. This is very similar to developing a high degree of emotional granularity. It comes because we practise, we pay attention, we notice – and we begin to get a real internal feel for the subtle differences in our internal motivations. It is not something that we can put off until we are faced with a major career choice, or deciding whether to begin a particular relationship. We need to start right where we are, with the small things that we face on a daily basis. We must begin by looking at our understanding of life. If we are to take faith seriously there is only one possible starting point for each of us, and that is exactly where we are right now.

The purpose of life is to allow relationship with God to develop and deepen to such an extent that the desire to serve God takes precedence over all other desires. In *The Spiritual Exercises* Ignatius talks about disordered affections: desires are important, but if any desire is placed above the desire for relationship with God we get ourselves into trouble. As we come to know and trust that we are *loved as we are*, with all the baggage and complications that we bring, we discover that we are called by God, exactly as we are, to be a part of the establishment of love in our world. In the midst of this, we are journeying with Jesus through his life, coming to know him, and allowing him to know us. We discover in the deepening relationship that a better, more generous, more loving, more dynamic version of ourselves is beginning to emerge.

In this deepening relationship we no longer feel the compulsion to hide our temptations. And we discover, too, in revealing our disordered desires and destructive tendencies, that their power over us diminishes. More importantly, we begin to discover a God who is not shocked by the fact that we do not always choose the better path. We discover a God who walks with us wherever we go. We discover a God who always desires the best for us. In all of this, we begin to glimpse the truth that, if we put relationship with God first, the self that emerges will be the most authentic version of ourselves – and the self we most like and are most happy to be. To put relationship with God first is no chore, no sacrifice; it is profoundly resonant with the very depths of our being. Putting relationship with God first is in its deepest essence choosing a life of meaning and purpose.

If relationship with God is put first then the way in which I live my life will be permeated, on all levels, by this fundamental attitude. The work I do, the relationships I have, the way in which I live, the way in which I interact with the world will all be influenced. My vocation, my fundamental call, is into relationship with God. Once that is in place, I will have the capacity, when necessary, to discern between the good and the better.

It should be noted though that there is no guarantee that on any given occasion I will actually choose the better over the good. In the same way, even in my closest personal relationships, I am not always sufficiently self-aware, let alone sufficiently generous, to choose that which is best for the relationship over that which serves my immediate personal needs. I still have a capacity to make choices which are less than loving.

Once I have discovered the God who knows the very best and very worst of me, and loves me, and I have discovered that this God, with all this knowledge, calls me not simply as a foot soldier but as a beloved companion. I am more willing to risk indifference, in the Ignatian sense, because I know that fundamentally God is utterly *for* me. Indifference in the Ignatian sense is a willingness to pay attention to my desires, to allow them to grow and deepen in the knowledge that I may be asked to set that desire aside to pursue the more important desire of relationship with God. Although we believe that God wants the best for us, many of us have grown up with rather bizarre ideas of God's intentions for us. It is common to think that the hardest road is the one most valued by God. With a God who is utterly for us, that which is best for the world and best for me are unlikely to be mutually exclusive. From the point of understanding that our principal purpose is relationship with God, all other things, in so far as they are good, should be held in balance. This means that we should be as willing to follow the call to a life of wealth, as to one of indigence; to a life of health, as to one of sickness; to a life honoured, as to one overlooked.

Living discernment

In *The Spiritual Exercises* Ignatius is careful to distinguish between those kinds of decisions which can be overturned and those which are more permanent. An obvious example of the more permanent kind of decision would be marriage and (though we may not feel euphoric about it every minute of every day) we are not likely to expend too much psychic energy worrying about the choice we made. Smaller, more arbitrary, choices can be different: habitually second-guessing ourselves over the less consequential decisions we've made can get in the way of the living of life.

I have long said that I wish to live with no regrets. I want to make each decision that I come to with prayer and discernment, so that at each juncture I can be confident that I made the choice that I believed I was called to, regardless of how that choice actually works out. Hindsight is not helpful. If, in making a decision, I fail to educate myself as fully as possible, given the constraints of time, energy and resources, then I have cause for regret. If I fail to inquire sufficiently and am caught by some circumstance which I could reasonably have known about beforehand and which would have altered my decision, it is reasonable to lament such a decision. However, if I do what I can and pray and discern and then choose a particular road, and that road turns out to be different from the one I had anticipated – and quite possibly harder – I may have better information for my next decision, and certainly I should have no cause for regret. We cannot predict how things will work out; we must step forward in faith. But stepping forward in faith does not require us to be either naïve or uninformed. This relationship with God that we have discovered, and which is to be an ongoing life process, requires that we bring our whole selves to the table. We need to use the resources we have available; they are all part of the discernment process.

Discernment versus decision-making

It has been argued by some that any decision made by a person who practises Ignatian spirituality should be a discerned one. Once the fundamental choice has been made that deepening relationship with God is the core motivation in my life, then everything else is weighed according to whether this particular avenue is congruent with that fundamental desire or not. If following this path gets in the way of deepening encounter with God, then why would I choose it, whatever merits it may have? Alternatively, if this path facilitates deepening encounter with God, then no matter what challenges it offers, it is probably a good path to take. At this level, the thing to notice is the trajectory – does this path lead me closer to God or not? There is no qualitative difference between this choice and the myriad choices we make daily and reflect upon in the examen.

Regardless of our good intentions and our careful discernment, we will occasionally end up on paths which lead us away from God. The key in this situation is simply to recognise the truth and to make the internal one hundred and eighty degree swivel. We cannot 'unmake' choices already made. We cannot go back in time. All we can do is examine ourselves and notice where we went wrong. Perhaps some personal baggage swayed our decision. Perhaps the decision was absolutely right, but in living it out we allowed ourselves to get distracted by secondary attachments. All we can do is notice that we have allowed ourselves to get distracted, and focus once again on God. Whilst I believe that poor discernment is a relatively common occurrence, and we can all learn to discern more accurately, I am not sure that such a thing as a 'wrong' decision is possible. Recall that at this level we are discerning between two good paths, one of which is likely to be better than the other. Neither path, of itself, is likely to cost us our integrity.

When we discover that our discernment was a little off, we can examine the method we used, try to isolate weak areas, and attempt to resolve these weaknesses in the future. An example of a weak area would be in giving either too much or too little weight to the opinions of others. But God is infinitely resourceful and can cope very well with us wherever we may be, regardless of the quality of any discernment we may have made in the past. Even if we want to, we cannot retrace our steps and make the decision again. What is done is done. All we can do is find God in our current reality and consciously allow God to take the central role in our lives once again. Today is a new day and we really do get a fresh start. This is not to suggest though that we are free of the consequences of the choices we have made. It is useful again to call to mind the metaphor Gerry O'Mahoney SJ uses of a person walking down the road: if you notice you're looking into your own shadow, just turn until you catch sight of God again. The point is simply that even if you feel that you have messed up or made a mistake, you can still find God from exactly where you are.

'Times' of making a decision

In *The Spiritual Exercises* Ignatius describes three different processes by which we make decisions. He calls these 'different times of making an election[38]'. The 'first time' occurs

---

38   Michael Ivens (2006) [175–177]

when you just know. 'When God our Lord so moves and at-tracts the will that without doubting or being able to doubt, the faithful soul follows what is shown[39].' Somehow, from some internal depth, there is a sense of just knowing that this is right. And that internal knowing does not change with the passage of time, or the introduction of new information.

The 'second time' occurs 'when sufficient light and knowl-edge is received through the experience of consolations and desolations, and through the experience of discernment of spirits[40].' In this second time, there is far more tussling and weighing up of different elements. There is much more active conscious discernment. A passage of time is implicit in the phrase 'experience of consolations and desolations'. We take the time to see where the spirits are actually leading. Time is an important factor in discerning between that which is truly good and that which looks good. As time progresses we find ourselves moved in different ways. If we are attentive to the movement of the Spirit of God, and we continue to seek God in all things, the dust will settle and the way forward will become clear. But it requires patience, perseverance and a commitment to finding that which God is truly asking of us.

There is no turbulent movement of spirits when the 'third time' occurs, but it is usually accompanied by some time pressure. We have to make a decision about what to do next and there is no strong affective sense of which path is better. It is the rational elements that provide the food for consid-eration rather than the noticing of the movements of spirits.

Following the description of the three times of making an election – the three ways in which we may be called to make a choice – Ignatius gives us advice on how to make a good election in the third time. It is important to note that this material, which is sometimes presented as Ignatius' advice

---

39   Michael Ivens (2006) [175]

40   Michael Ivens (2006) [176]

on making decisions, is applicable only to *the third time* of making a decision. A full discussion will follow, but for the moment suffice to say that this material focuses on teasing out the rational reasons for making a decision, and seeks to evoke some emotional affect as well. This point is important: a decision made in the third time is not discerned in the technical sense. Discernment is a sifting of the movements of spirits. In the third time, the spirits do not appear to be moving – usually because of an external pressure, such as time – so some other means of reaching a decision must be used. But discernment is a far better way to make a decision, so the second time is preferable to the third. It has been suggested that the very purpose of the extra material Ignatius gives in the third time is to get the spirits to move, or to reveal the movement of the spirits – to elicit some emotional response, shifting the decision into a second time mode, thereby allowing discernment to become the modus operandi.

It may be worthwhile illustrating the three times of making an election with some personal examples. As an election in the first time: my first experience around the job at Loyola Hall. Once I had spoken to the director, Paul Nicholson SJ, and the job was a real possibility, I knew that this was exactly what I wanted and it seemed entirely consistent with the trajectory of my being up until that point. I had no doubts that this was absolutely right and in line with God's will for me. There was no weighing up of alternatives, it was simply right.

As an election in the second time: making the decision to take a postdoc in France at the end of my PhD. As a result of making the Spiritual Exercises and with a growing desire to follow my sense of calling, I had been absolutely sure that I would be leaving chemistry after I finished my PhD. I had no desire to spend any more time in a research lab and I was certain that my call was into spirituality. I met Prof Jacques Brocard in February 2002 and I was due to submit my thesis by the end of June of that year. I had made plans to go to Loyola Hall to train in spiritual direction in February 2003. A week or so after I met Jacques he sent me an email offering me a postdoctoral research position in his lab in France. Initially, I felt certain that I did not want it, but it would have been rude to dismiss the offer without at least the appearance of consideration, so I entered into a correspondence where I asked questions and received responses over a period of a couple of weeks. The offer was for a six month contract – normally postdocs are for at least a year – he could organise accommodation for me; he would pay me well, and so on. As the days and weeks rolled by I found myself softening to the idea, and slowly I found myself actually wanting to accept. More importantly, I got the distinct feeling that this might be what God wanted too. It was truly bizarre. I wrestled back and forth several times, until finally I found myself sitting on my bed praying one morning, saying to God 'I am going to have to say yes to this, so if I am wrong, you are going to have to make it very clear to me.' In the couple of hours that passed between that prayer period and actually accepting the position, I received two strong indicators confirming that I was doing the right thing. Throughout the process there were strong feelings at work. In allowing myself to seriously consider the possibility, new information stirred my internal movements, my own feelings changed completely and I ended up making an active conscious discernment that was truly surprising to me.

As an election in the third time: making the decision to leave school teaching and go to UCT to do Honours in Chemistry. After completing my undergraduate degree I spent a year teaching maths at St George's College, a Jesuit school in Harare. This year of teaching was precipitated by the fact I had wanted to do medicine but that had not worked out. I was happy teaching; I really enjoyed my life and my job, but I had already applied to UCT to do Honours in Chemistry. At this point I knew nothing about 'discernment'; I thought that doing Honours would be a good idea but I had no strong feelings about the process. In the end, I made the decision based on an idea I had of taking the 'path of least regret.' I knew that I could return to teaching at some later date if I wanted to, but the opportunity to do Honours, and the bursary I had been offered, was a once-off thing.

Aids for making a decision in the Third Time

It is important to reiterate here the significant difference between making an election in the first and second times, and making one in the third time. Ignatius is confident that when there is distinct movement of spirits, provided we are actively discerning, we will be fine. We will come to a good decision, because, even if we initially opt for the lesser choice, we will notice, sooner or later, that something is 'off'. For the election in the third time, we have no such information.

Here Ignatius uses two main tools. The first is the 'four column' method: reasons for A, reasons against A, reasons for B and reasons against B. This is better than the usual pro and con list because the reasons for A and the reasons against B may not necessarily be the same. It helps to clarify the thinking.

The second 'tool' is slightly more melodramatic. Imagine yourself giving advice to your best friend on this decision – what do you find yourself arguing? Or imagine yourself on your deathbed – what do you wish you had done?

Final comments

In all of this, the foundation of making good, discerned decisions is the practice of the examen. Beginning to notice what really moves you each day is a vital start to the whole process. We cannot possibly think that we will be able to discover what God truly desires for us if we do not take the time to get to know ourselves, to allow our desires to make themselves known. We need to pay attention to the still, small voice within, to notice the nudging and leaning that is within us. Otherwise we may find ourselves leaping at the first option we come across that looks vaguely attractive. We need to give God time to show us what God wants; sometimes it can be quite surprising. But God will work with our desires; God will not ask us to do things that are totally out of character. Sometimes we will be challenged to step beyond our comfort zone, but such invitations tend to be expansive not oppressive. They lead us to the discovery that we are far more than we thought we were. Finally, do not forget that it is entirely possible that your deepest desire is God's desire for you; and that what is best for the world may also be best for you.

Do you have examples of decisions you have made in the first, second and third times?

In your first or second time choices, how have you experienced God's communication to you?

Do you have people you go to when you have choices to make?

Do you have a choice to make at the moment?

What is your desire?

What seems to be God's desire for you?

Are there any other factors you need to consider?

What happens when you hold it all in conversation with God?

Chapter 9: Finding Your Purpose

Happiness, I have come to understand, comes when
what I choose to be about in life is actually
worth spending my life doing
— Joan Chittister OSB

When you consider your work, your relationships, your hobbies – is your life worth the investment?

How passionate do you feel about the things that you do?

Does it feel as if you are making a contribution to the world?

Is what you do important to you, or are you focused simply on making enough money to be able to play the way you want to?

Pause and talk to God about your life a little.

We live in a world where work is by and large a means to an end. Work provides a way to fund our lifestyle. In as much as we have choices, most of us will tend to choose fields of work which are of some personal interest, or at least in alignment with our talents and abilities, and if these can be readily combined with something that is reasonably lucrative, so much the better. For many people the question of the purpose of work stops there. This attitude is nothing new:

> [Work] should be looked upon, not as a necessary drudgery to be undergone for the purpose of making money, but as a way of life in which the nature of man should find its proper exercise and delight and so fulfill itself to the glory of God[41].

---

41   Dorothy Sayers (1974) p.89.

This quotation is from a paper delivered by author Dorothy Sayers in about 1940 and I am sure the idea was not new then. There are a significant number of self-help style books which are dedicated to the question of finding our passion in life. Nevertheless, it is still relatively rare to find people who feel that they have been *called* to their particular job, even if they enjoy what they do.

I think that there are a number of different reasons why people are happy to settle for a pay cheque rather than a sense of purpose. There are those who are genuinely satisfied with doing a job which gives them sufficient income to live as they want to. 'Living as they want to' usually comprises some combination of hobbies, travel and children. Their choice of job will be dictated to by the size of the pay cheque, the benefits and the convenience of the work arrangements. They will give little thought as to the nature of the company for which they will be working. This is not to say that these people are necessarily driven by a desire for status or material wealth, rather the question of purpose just does not seem to be important. For most of you who have got this far into this book, the question of purpose is likely to be lurking somewhere in your being. For some, the question will just be emerging, there will be a sense that it is an important question to consider, but a way into the question may not yet be clear. For others, there may seem to be a clear answer to the question, but it will require making life changes which are difficult to implement. But for most people there will be a sense that this question has been around for a while and that you are living into the answer. It is also true that for many of us the task of living is all-consuming. This is particularly true for those who have young children; we do not seem to have much leisure to question our life's purpose.

Why is the question important?

I have recently come across a few articles on the regrets of the dying. All of them seem to have the same source – Bronnie Ware, author of *The Top Five Regrets of Dying*[42]. They vary slightly in wording and ordering but essentially all seem to point to similar themes. These are the top five:

> I wish I had had the courage to be true to myself and my dreams, rather than live to expectations of others
>
> I wish I had invested more in my relationships with family and friends
>
> I wish I hadn't worked so hard
>
> I wish I had been able to express my feelings
>
> I wish I had let myself be happier

As we consider these regrets, the significance of the question of purpose may become a little clearer. It is not a question we can easily put off. Many of us feel a sense of discomfort or frustration at the status quo, and it is better to channel the energy of this dissatisfaction into asking the fundamental questions rather than into fuelling our distractions.

As we navigate the world of figuring out what it is we are supposed to be doing, it is important to recognise that what we do is only half of the picture. Our relationships are also a very important component of our purpose. Most of us will err on one side or the other. Some will tend to focus on their careers more than their relationships, others will choose relationships over their careers. As a generalisation, many people assume that men tend to focus on the former and women on the latter. As a woman who has only recently figured out the real importance of relationships, I would caution against an uncritical adoption of this bias. Certainly, the list of the top five regrets would suggest that it is better to err (if it is erring) on the side of focusing on relationships rather than on work. This is not particularly surprising in a culture which focuses so strongly on extrinsically measurable variables. It is important for each of us to understand our own inclinations and to recognise the importance of getting something

---

42   Bronnie Ware (2012).

of a balance between the work we do, on the one hand, and our relationships on the other. I would, therefore, caution against swallowing the 'regrets' list without some rumination.

If we are working only to earn money to sustain lifestyles fuelled by extrinsic motivation, our efforts may seem pretty meaningless at the end of our lives – because they are. Driving a Mercedes Benz does not guarantee that we will be happier than if we drove something more modest. Living in a mansion does not guarantee that we will be happier than if we lived in a small apartment. Once we earn sufficiently to be able to feed, clothe and educate our families, our happiness does not increase with an increasing size of pay cheque. So investing heavily in work simply so that we can play more, or have a luxury car or an expensive vacation, will give us a hit of hedonic contentment which is, of its nature, temporary. I recently encountered a couple who have focused on exotic vacations for many years. Now in their seventies, they are becoming bored with travel. Once the contentment has passed we cannot recreate it, and it has no real meaning. However, if we are involved in work that is meaningful to us, or gives us a sense of purpose, a sense that our contribution is in some way valuable, that sense of satisfaction is likely to be lasting.

There is now sufficient research on the factors which motivate people to show that remuneration beyond a certain basic level fails to provide incentive. Rather it is the sense of meaning or purpose which makes the difference, coupled with a sense of challenge. Most of us, who care to think about things, want a life that is worth living. That is to say, not simply a life that is enjoyable and comfortable, but a life of contribution. Exactly what a 'life of contribution' means will vary from person to person and it is precisely discerning what this means for each of us that is important. I've chosen to use the term 'discerning' rather than 'figuring out' in the previous sentence because it is a lifelong task. It is about finding the task that I am passionate about, able to do, for which I am qualified and which allows me to earn a living.

Some impediments

Finding our purpose is not easy. Whilst some people do have a very clear idea of what they are supposed to do from an early age, for most of us the process is far more organic. As we develop we encounter different potential paths, and different challenges. Each of these teaches us something about ourselves, something about our world and something about the way in which we interact with the world. Over time, we learn that we are naturally adept at some things and that we struggle with others. We find ourselves drawn down some avenues and gently pushed away by others. This is not to suggest that the path of least resistance is necessarily the best path to choose. Indeed, having a little adversity can contribute substantially to our internal resilience in ways which are invaluable in dealing with life.

The idea of purpose can easily be skewed unhelpfully by the institutional Church. Frequently there is an implicit understanding that things associated with the church somehow have greater value. For example, in the Roman Catholic Church this idea of life purpose is usually expressed in the word 'vocation'. We have an annual 'Vocations Sunday', a day on which we pray especially for vocations to the priesthood and the religious life. Whilst it is evident that for the perpetuation of the church, in its current form, we need people who will live out their lives in this way, to use the term 'vocation' as being synonymous with 'religious vocation' is detrimental to the sense of call of the vast majority of people who are called to other ways of life. I was very pleased on Vocations Sunday a couple of years ago to hear our parish priest supporting this idea of vocation in the broader sense. Dorothy Sayers put it even more strongly: 'In nothing has the Church so lost Her hold on reality as in Her failure to understand and respect the secular vocation[43].'

If we think about vocation or life purpose as being something that must be fixed and defined by a particular job we

---

43   Dorothy Sayers (1974) p.89.

are limiting ourselves. Life continually hands us different circumstances. We have no control over this. At one time I believed I was called to the religious life and made choices that were in keeping with that understanding. Pursuing that path led me, eventually, to Loyola Hall. I then spent time living in the reality of being a spiritual director. Because I took that as a calling, I gave myself fully to the process. In the end I found myself being called out of spirituality and back to chemistry. Was I mistaken in my initial sense of calling to religious life? Only if one narrowly defines 'correct' as indicating an ultimate outcome in perfect alignment with the initial call. A correct call, by this measure, would have meant that I became a religious sister. The truth is that, by asking the question of whether I was being called to the religious life, and by allowing discernment to continually shape my call, the lived reality of that calling has taken a very different shape. I would not be where I am – and, more importantly, *who* I am – today if I had not pursued that original call. I was as surprised as anyone else when I found myself being called directly back into the life I thought I had left behind.

A way of being

Vocation, in this broader sense, is fundamentally about seeking our unique contribution. That unique contribution will be the way in which we can develop most fully into our being, and it will also provide an avenue which is somehow of use to the world. It is important to understand that as humans, although we gain from input such as education and healthcare, we also gain from artistic expression and creativity. If we focus too much on the usefulness of our work rather than how well it fits our being, we can miss that which is our true vocation. I know someone who dropped out of medical school to take up music. Some might argue that the work of a doctor has more intrinsic value than that of a musician, but for this particular person the journey into the fullness of her being was better mediated by a career in music than one in medicine. Again discernment is at the heart of the process, with the important understanding that discernment is a complex and ongoing process.

The questions at the heart of it all are: 'Where can I be most fully myself?'; 'Where am I most fully alive?' At the end of our lives, if we are called to account in some way, we will probably not be questioned on what we 'did' or which organisations we belonged to, or the number of people we brought to faith. We will be asked if we had the courage to be fully ourselves. I firmly believe that if we try to be fully ourselves, if we try to seek God every day, and if we practise ongoing discernment, that we cannot help but fulfil our purpose. The purpose emerges naturally from living that discerned life. We will continue to receive invitations, some of which we will find ourselves choosing to respond to, some of which we will not. Invitations to step up wash over us continually; we do not have to go looking for them. If we are committed to discernment and to living authentically, we will not be able to stop ourselves from responding to some of the invitations. Remembering always that we are committed to that which will bring the *greater* glory of God – with the understanding that the glory of God is the human person fully alive. This means that that which brings glory to God will not be to the detriment of who we are.

Please note, this is not in any way to say that a path which leads one into conflict with authority, which results in imprisonment, torture, or some form of oppression or slander cannot be our call. To suggest that any form of hardship is somehow indicative of a failure to be faithful, or something along those lines would be utterly misguided. The fact is that we live in a broken world, and there are undoubtedly times when good, passionate people have been crushed by repressive systems. Indeed, how could we understand the Passion of Christ, if our measure of finding our vocation were merely the degree of extrinsic ease it might bring?

There is however, an internal sense of at-homeness, or happiness, or rightness which is associated with finding one's purpose, and living it. Joan Chittister in her book *Following the Path: The search for a life of passion, purpose and joy* has a beautiful description of the simplicity of this experience:

> I was just sitting, on an ordinary day in the midst of the ordinary things of life, waiting for a friend to arrive. And then it happened. The gentlest sense of wholeness and deep-down satisfaction came over me that I have ever known. It enfolded me like warm mist and calmed me to the core. Every ounce of taut energy so common to the demands of daily life in a technological society had been drained, it seemed. Only the feeling of being totally, quietly, completely alive remained. Then I realized what it was: I was happy. Happy. That's all. Just happy[44].

In the absence of clear purpose

If you do not have a sense of this kind of purpose – or feel you do not have it yet – and there is no clear pull in any obvious direction, it is probably most helpful to assume that you are in the place you need to be right now. In this case, commit yourself to doing what you do as well as you can. Become expert at the task at hand. Committing yourself to working in this way will, at the very least, bear good witness, and as you immerse yourself in what you do, you will find greater pleasure in it. Beyond that let God be God – and reveal the next step in God's good time.

Do you have a sense of purpose or vocation?

If you feel you are living that, then take a moment to give thanks to God.

Do you feel you are heading in the right direction even if it is not exactly clear to you what that will be?

Again, take a few moments to talk to God about where you are.

If you do not have that sense yet, talk to God about that too.

---

44   Joan Chittister (2012) p.14.

Chapter 10: When Things are Tough

He who learns must suffer. And even in our sleep, pain that cannot forget, falls drop by drop upon the heart, and in our own despair, against our will, comes wisdom to us by the awful grace of God

— Aeschylus

N o matter how well we choose, and how well we live our lives, things go wrong. It is important to have some idea of things that can help us ride out the storms that will cross our paths.

....

When you think about some of the difficulties you have encountered in your life, do you have a sense of God's presence with you in the process?

Do you try to integrate managing challenges with your image of God?

Pause. Who is the God that you are aware of as you begin this chapter?

The purpose of this chapter is not to attempt to answer the problem of evil in the world, nor to throw my ten cents' worth into existing theodicy arguments. The uncomfortable, inescapable reality is that we cannot live in our world and fail to be visited by death, by painful relationships, by violence. We will face fear, we will face disappointment and we will face rejection. For some of us, those experiences are far more a part of our lives than for others. Grappling with the question of how God can be a loving God and yet allow these things to happen is one of the rites of passage to a mature relationship with God. It is also a question which many of us return to again and again as we are faced with new challenges.

Struggles can challenge our image of God

In the chapter on images of God (Chapter 2) I raised the idea of the spiritual schizophrenia that many of us suffer from – a deep-seated fear of God, juxtaposed with a continual expression of just how loving God is. Overcoming that hurdle, to discover that God is truly loving, is the most important transition of our lives of faith. Nonetheless, sooner or later, once we have come to truly believe in the depths of our being that God is loving, something will happen that will shake that faith. In the world in which we live it is inevitable that we will be confronted with some injustice, some pain, some natural disaster which makes us question everything that we thought we knew about God. In the abstract that may sound a little scary, if you have not already experienced it. So let me give another personal example.

In September 2002, I had been living in France for all of ten days, when my dad was arrested in Zimbabwe. As was fairly standard in Zimbabwe at the time, he was arrested early on Friday morning, as Saturday and Sunday do not count towards the forty-eight hours before charges must be brought. It was also standard practice that the person's whereabouts would be buried in bureaucratic minutiae. These tactics are designed to create the greatest stress possible within the constraints of the letter of the law. A little background to the story is that my dad was a judge. Just before he retired he sentenced the Minister of Justice to three months in jail for contempt of court. Legally speaking, this was the appropriate sentence under the circumstances. Needless to say, the Zimbabwean Government was not terribly pleased with this, and they created some allegations against my dad for which they arrested him and later charged him.

That period was terribly difficult for the whole family, but I will speak only of my own experience. I had been at home when my dad had made the decision to sentence the minister, and I was aware that this was difficult decision for him, knowing that it could well have unpleasant consequences. From my perspective, I believed that he was taking a stand for justice. The weekend he was arrested, I found myself struggling to pray. By that stage in my life I had had a good experience of God's love for me. I understood God to be a loving God. Nonetheless, that Saturday afternoon, as I walked through the fields on the outskirts of the small village where I was staying, I found myself at an impasse. If I prayed that no charges be brought against my dad – as I truly believed was right and just and in accordance with the will of God – what would I do if the outcome was not as I had prayed it would be? But why on earth would God not intervene in such clear circumstances? The choice to act had been discerned (or so it appeared to me), and the action had been just. How then could God possibly allow punishment?

Did I even want a relationship with a God who would not act in such circumstances?

In the end, I found I had to pray, because if I chose not to pray at that stage, I would have already been making a choice – I would have been stepping out of relationship with God without allowing God a chance to respond. So how did it turn out? Well, not as we had hoped. My dad was charged with corruption and we faced nine more months of tension before the start of his trial. On the morning the trial was due to begin, the charges were dropped prior to a plea. During those nine months I found myself really questioning whether I believed in God at all. How on earth was it possible that such suffering was permitted after such a difficult, but good, choice had been made?

Ultimately, as I grappled with this tension, I began to realise the truth of the statement: 'I do not pray because it changes God, I pray because it changes me'. In this case, what I had prayed for was not granted, but in being true to myself and what I desired in prayer I ended up grappling with my images of God and my understanding of God's action in the world. This engagement fundamentally changed the way in which I approach my faith. God has not changed in the process, but I have. We really do not understand why bad things happen, and in the midst of the chaos of the pain, it is impossible to see that there might be some grace in the midst of it. Nonetheless, God is a loving God, and ultimately God sits with us in the pain and suffering. It is crucially important for the development of a mature faith that we learn to be honest with God in the midst of the chaos.

I do not believe – as some do – that God visits suffering upon us to make us stronger, in the same way that I do not believe that the pain and suffering of the cross was somehow *necessary* for our redemption. I believe that we live in a broken world; a world where suffering and pain is handed on from one generation to the next, unconsciously and unceasingly. Some of life's tragedies can be explained through human sin – for example, greed and a lust for power give rise to all sorts of personal injury. Many of the chronic diseases we suffer can be attributed, at least in part, to the toxicity of our environment or our emotional being. But some tragedies cannot be attributed to any human activity – the 2011 earthquake and tsunami in Japan is just one such example. Sometimes over-zealous pastors try to explain natural disasters in terms of God's righteous anger and a purging of society – such as the voices which claimed that Hurricane Katrina was God's judgement upon the wanton lifestyle of some of the people of New Orleans. Such messages are not helpful. They give an image of a vengeful God willing to wreak havoc to prove a point. I simply cannot believe in such a God, and I cannot believe that the Creator of the Universe could not think of more wholesome ways to teach us lessons. However – and this is a big however – I do believe that God can use any situation as a vehicle for grace.

Engaging with pain

In *The Spiritual Exercises*, Ignatius takes us through a process of engaging with pain. We are invited in the Third Week to pray for the grace to experience being with Christ in sorrow. The Third Week focuses on the Passion of Christ – we walk with him, as a companion from the entry to Jerusalem to death on the cross. The Fourth Week of the Exercises is a contemplation on the resurrection; the grace we pray for is joy with Christ in joy. A fascinating thing about the dynamic of the Third and Fourth Weeks of the Exercises is how inextricably they are linked. Sœur Anne Peyremoite, who was my spiritual director when I was in France, once commented that we can cry our way through the Third Week without fully engaging with it because we have all known pain, but we cannot fake the Fourth Week's joy. The joy comes only if we have actually engaged with the pain.

Engaging with pain does not mean that we need to wallow unnecessarily in it, but we do have to explore it, and allow ourselves to be vulnerable to it. There is an important difference between reflective rumination and ruminative brooding. Reflective rumination is an intentional internal engagement with what has happened. It gives rise to an emotionally intelligent response and may include a resolution to action. Ruminative brooding is a self-destructive fascination with the pain. It does not lead to growth or action, but rather results in paralysis. A Jesuit priest, Fr Laplace, once observed that the Third and Fourth Weeks of the Exercises are like two pools interconnected only at the deepest point. The joy of the resurrection comes when we have fully immersed ourselves in the pain of the crucifixion. In everyday life, I think this means that we need to allow ourselves to feel our pain, to be vulnerable to its depths, before we can begin to glimpse the grace that it might conceal.

Allowing pain to shape us

Pain often shifts our internal contours. We are forced to let
go of some things and to rethink others. It is well known that
going through an experience of trauma is likely to result in
the questioning of our belief system. This questioning may
include the nature of God, the nature of the world and our
own self-understanding. It is often scary because it can feel
as though we are losing our sense of self. In a way we are, we
are losing the way in which we have understood our world
and it is part of human nature to resist such change. But if
we are able to sit in it, and to talk to God about it, to rage at
God at the unfairness of it all, and to weep with God for what
we have lost; if we dare to be honest with God in the process, sooner or later we will begin to discover a sense of joy.
A joy which has no external source, rather, it is the joy which
comes from the fiery purging of pain; the joy which comes
from allowing our presumptions about our world to be challenged and re-shaped. Once we have said what we need to
say, if we can sit for a moment longer than is comfortable
with the detritus of what we thought we knew to be true,
something shifts. Like the pastures in Namaqualand in the
spring, an unexpected burst of colour enters our world. We
discover our experience to be shot through with grace.

In five years a lifetime has passed.
Our lives today so different –
no clear trajectory
has brought us to this place.
The journey travelled much further
than the distance covered.
Whilst I wouldn't choose this route again
I wouldn't trade where we are now
for where we were then.
Yes, we were happy, contented, optimistic,
much as we seem to be today.
But we have discovered redemption.

We have learned that pain
can be a gift,
that calamity can give us courage.
We are more loving,
more compassionate.
We have discovered our vulnerability
and find that it is our greatest strength.
We have no capacity to control life,
but we have discovered the power of choice.
In life-seeking response
comes resurrection[45].

If we do not process the pain, we will end up bitter and disappointed, wondering what happened, what went wrong. Processing pain is not easy, and it does not happen quickly. But the cost of failing to grapple with it is so much greater.

We have a choice when we are confronted with the brutality of the world. We can erect a wall around the most vulnerable parts of our being, protecting it against the pain and suffering. The problem with this approach is that we cannot do this and love. We cannot know the joy of love and be protected from pain. If we are to know love we must be vulnerable to hurt.

A word of caution: do not try to 'learn the lesson' too soon

When we hear about 'the stages of grief' or 'the stages of forgiveness' we are likely to presume that these processes are linear. One travels from denial through anger to bargaining, on to depression and finally to acceptance. But the reality is that the road to healing is a long and winding one. Around

---

45   Margaret Blackie (2008) p.123.

each corner new vistas emerge. Or sometimes old ones appear unexpectedly. On some turns we are confronted again with raw emotion – as though nothing has changed and no time has passed. It seems that we have made no progress whatsoever, when just hours before we had felt almost normal again. This is both turbulent and tiring. But if we dare to pause for a moment in the chaos, and allow ourselves to feel the pain again, to talk to God and to acknowledge our loss and our pain, we find it has shifted a little. If we do this, and do not simply try to distract ourselves, we find that, as time progresses, the frequency with which we revisit the raw emotion slowly diminishes – though it may take many passes through those dark passages before the contours of soul are remoulded.

Brené Brown, in her book *The Gifts of Imperfection*, writes of the importance of 'trying to feel the feelings, staying mindful about numbing behaviours, and trying to lean into the discomfort of hard emotions[46]'. I would add to that brief list that we need to be discerning. We need to be vigilant about what is leading us towards God, what is leading to a greater sense of self, and what is diminishing that. We need to recognise that the appropriate choice will vary from day to day – or even during the course of a single day. It may be exactly the right thing to feel the feelings in the morning, but if that becomes overwhelming and threatens to drown us, choosing some healthy numbing behaviour (as described in the introduction to this book) later in the day may be totally appropriate. Ultimately most of us will try to avoid actually experiencing the discomfort of hard emotions, which is why I really like the expression 'trying to lean into the discomfort of hard emotions'. I am not advocating a wholesale undiscerning plunge into the darkness; rather an attitude of willingness to really grapple with the tough stuff.

---

46   Brené Brown (2010) p.69.

It may take longer than you think it ought to

Many years ago I was emotionally assaulted – at least that is how I experienced it. Without having expressed previously any dissatisfaction with my performance, two people very much older than me took an action that was a pointed public criticism of the way in which I had performed in a particular role. I am certain they did not intend the extent of damage they caused, but I think it is fair to say that they did intend to make a specific point through their actions. At the time I simply swallowed my feelings, and moved on – or so I thought. About a year later I found myself overwhelmed by a sense of anger, so I sat down and wrote one of them a letter. There was no reply, but I believed that bringing the issue to light had somehow healed my hurt. But some years after that I was surprised to discover that I hadn't dealt fully with what had happened, and I processed it again, as best as I could. Years later, however, I was reprimanded when a task I had been instructed to do caused difficulties for some colleagues, and again memories of that initial wounding flooded my mind. Yet more years went by and another set of circumstances – hearing second-hand of a complaint about my behaviour – triggered the old emotions. Then, after several more years had passed – seventeen by now since the original hurt – something completely new opened up the old fault-line. Each time I tried to put the problem to rest as best I could. Each time I looked on what had happened with fresh eyes. Each time understood a little better. But still it remained.

Finally, in 2011, I was subject to a very angry email from someone whom I had hurt significantly over a decade before. I found myself wondering how long we can justifiably hold on to personal hurt, and how we are to know when is it time to let go. As I read his letter I realised the writer was lashing out at the person I had been more than ten years before. I have learnt a lot since then. I probably wouldn't make the same choices today – in part precisely because of the hurt that I had caused him. The point here is that the people who hurt me so long ago are probably also no longer the same people. They too have had many years of living since then; it would be truly surprising if they hadn't changed at all in that time. I can no longer hold the people they are today responsible for their actions back then. I have had to let go of the sense of blame. I realised at last that carrying the blame had been crippling me – and that it was time to let it go. The two people involved may never realise that I had held them with such anger and in such contempt for so long, but I believe on some level that the releasing of that tension will have been good for all three of us. Even the law acknowledges the significance of the passage of time, and with it the gain of life experience. With the exception of murder, there is a statute of limitations on crime – a time after which it is no longer legally possible to hold a person responsible for actions carried out much earlier in life. I recognise now that I was in a particularly vulnerable space when the original incident happened; at some other time I might have processed the hurt far more easily. So please note that I not talking here about sustained physical or emotional abuse – in cases where there has been substantial trauma, the passage of time without professional help may not be sufficient to give access to real healing.

Knowledge is dangerous.
I am beginning to understand
the extent of the paralysis
caused by events of the past.
I think I have finally identified the ghosts.
I recognise the web of sin
that has trapped my body and soul.
I know that in such recognition
lies my redemption.
But memories stir
and a gamut of emotion is evoked.
I know my mind has distorted
the original events, and they

are now frozen in a place beyond truth,
the twisted facts layered over by
years of crippled response.
Who said what to whom
and who did what when
is no longer the key to
disarm the tangled mess.
In the midst of it all
salvation comes in an unlikely guise.
A man, a god, holding it all together,
holding us all together –
in the tortuous silence of unnamed grief.
He was there all along, and none of us knew.
The tangled web of grief and hurt,
of silence and deceit,
bind him more strongly to us
than the nails in the crucifix –
the pain no less agonising.
But there is hope,
there will be redemption.
I am still ensnared
but that consciousness releases power.
The scars will remain
but the paralysis is receding.
In the meantime while movement returns
and the blood flow is restored
the tissue cries out in agony.
Redemption comes
at great cost[47].

---

47   Margaret Blackie (2008) p.121.

Numbing behaviour

I wrote briefly, at the beginning of this book about healthy – useful – 'numbing behaviour'. Within the context of the attempt to deal with things, it can be useful to engage in activities which remind us of normal life. Dealing with painful issues needs energy and attention, and this requires that we find healthy ways to have timeout from the immediacy of pain. We all participate, at some time, in numbing behaviours of one sort or another. As I explained previously, there is nothing wrong with this, indeed, it can be a lifeline of sanity in our world.

Numbing behaviours may be anything from a glass of wine in the evening, to exercise, to watching television, reading crime novels, knitting, playing Sudoku, even to becoming very involved in church life! Some numbing behaviours are potentially more toxic than others, and, for the most part, any numbing behaviour can escalate into some form of addiction or compulsion. The glass of wine example is a good one here – if you are not sure whether you use alcohol as a numbing tool, consider entering into a social scenario where alcohol is present, and not drinking. Similarly with food: imagine opening a bar of chocolate or a packet of crisps and having just one or two bites and then putting it down. If your activity is in the addiction or compulsion range, it is no longer healthy numbing behaviour. The most important consideration with numbing behaviour is whether it is conscious or not. Conscious engagement in some form of numbing activity is healthy. It gives us a way to step back from the immediacy of the hard emotions that are threatening to drown us, and it can allow us to take a breath and to gather strength before re-engaging.

But it is important to understand that numbing activity numbs everything. You cannot selectively numb the pain or grief or anger, you will numb the joy and, I believe, the spiritual consolation as well. This is where the distinction between conscious numbing and unconscious numbing becomes so important. Unconscious numbing is avoidance, whilst conscious numbing is the equivalent of taking a breather. But numbing behaviour can also numb spiritual consolation, so this avoidance may make God very hard to find.

So the first question to think about is: What are your numbing activities? Which of them seem to you to be inherently healthier? Watching television or going for a walk may offer the same level of numbing, but it is important for our overall sense of well-being that at least occasionally we are able to choose the healthier option. Also, if we are aware of the numbing behaviour that we usually choose, then we are far more likely to be able to make space for the real engagement that also needs to happen.

It is important here to be discerning – we need to pay attention to what happens when we participate in various numbing activities. There are some important questions to ask. Firstly, at the end of the activity (however enjoyable it has been) do I feel better or worse? Secondly, at the end of each day, which activities facilitate engagement with the thing I am struggling with, and which dampen my desire to engage? The former are useful numbing activities, the latter are really avoidance. There is a third question: have I caught a glimpse of God anywhere today? Healthy numbing will enable engagement with God; avoidance will not. So we start with the awareness that to truly process new circumstances, and to live into them, is something that takes a long time.

In the midst of it

So in the end, where are we? Pain is one of the awful realities of our world. We have probably all been on the receiving end of pain, but if we pause even briefly we are likely to see that we have spread pain too. It is our responsibility to minimise the damage we cause. For most of us the damage we cause arises out of parts of ourselves which have themselves been damaged. Oftentimes we are not even aware of the harm we have done. It requires humility, grace – and a willingness to allow God to reveal our woundedness – for us to begin to address this.

When we're struggling, we have to allow ourselves to experience the pain – to let God's grace work in us and through us. And we need to be honest with God. As Dermot Preston SJ, my spiritual director for several years, once said: God has broad shoulders! God can cope with our questions and our frustrations and our fears. If we fail to communicate honestly with God during these difficult periods, our relationship with God is likely to get stuck. And if that happens, we will not be able to grow in faith and love; we will not be transformed, because there is a no-go area in our conversation with God: an area into which we refuse to invite God because we are afraid of what it will mean. CS Lewis once wrote something to the effect that even your friends know when your mind is not fully on the conversation you are having with them – so how do we think we can fool God when we try to do that? When we tell God how wonderful God is, when actually we are raging internally at the injustice of what has happened, we are doing exactly this. It amounts to being two-faced with God. We wouldn't tolerate it if someone was doing that in conversation with us, so why would we think it's a good option in our communication with God?

Hope

Redemption is possible in any circumstance. Another way of saying this is to borrow from St Paul: 'All things can work to the good for those who love God.' God's grace truly is sufficient to cover all human experience. But we have to participate with God in this. We need to dare to be honest in prayer, and we need to be willing to be changed in the process. If those two prerequisites are in place, the transformation which can take place is truly astounding. Bitterness can be replaced by generosity, and anger by compassion.

The more frequently you see the transformative power of grace working through pain, the more you learn to trust it; the more you learn to risk sitting in the pain with God. Remember too, that after the resurrection, Jesus still bore the marks of the wounds. If we allow pain to paralyse us, we will inevitably sow seeds of destruction around us; but if we allow pain to transform us, our lives will become examples of the good news.

What are your numbing behaviours? When do they devolve into avoidance?

Are there areas in your life where, with hindsight, you can see that something that was tremendously painful has become the source of grace?

Does your image of God extend to a God who will sit with you in times of pain?

As you read this is there an invitation to talk to God about an area of difficulty in your life?

Chapter 11: Dealing with Hurts in Personal Relationships

Forgiveness is the key to action and freedom
— Hannah Arendt

Dealing with pain in life is sometimes directly associated with conflict in relationships. It is worth addressing this as a separate section because it is a often more complicated since there are always at least two parties involved.

●●

This chapter combines some of the material covered in Chapter 10 (on dealing with life difficulties) and some of the material covered in Chapter 5 (on praying for grace). I have included this chapter because hurts associated with the breakdown in relationships cause a particular kind of problem. The person with whom we are in conflict has been a part of our lives – and we of theirs – in some way, and we are faced with questions of whether to continue in the relationship or not. (Note here that I am using 'relationship' to mean any kind of interaction.)

Regardless of how we choose to proceed with respect to the relationship itself, we usually also have some kind of internal work to do in the process of forgiveness. I believe forgiveness is a grace to be prayed for – as alluded to in Chapter 5. Forgiveness is not something we can will ourselves into. It requires sifting through the detritus of the painful interaction to determine what fault is mine and what belongs to the other person. It requires discernment to see where I have been hooked by my own 'stuff' and where projection and transference have escalated emotions. It takes time and a willingness to let go of our self-righteousness. It takes the grace of God to untangle the interior mess. And it takes generosity to step beyond myself and reach out again to the other.

A personal disclaimer

Resolving difficulties in personal relationships is probably one of the most challenging subjects to write about. At least it is for me. It is challenging for me because I know that, even as I am typing these words, there are two truths which erode my confidence. The first is that I know without doubt that there are people out there who have not had a good experience of me. The second is that there are people who have hurt me whom I would rather never see again. I write this not from the place of one who has it all sorted out, but rather from the place of one who reflects deeply on things, who strives to see the truth and to learn from all things in life. I write aware of my failures, both those that are truly mine and those that have been attributed to me through misunderstandings. I dare to write, nevertheless, because in my quest for authenticity I believe that I have learnt some things along the way that may be helpful to others. I do not pretend to have all the answers and I certainly do not offer any magic formulae.

On the positive side, I have learnt an enormous amount from my experiences of failing in personal relationships, and there are areas in which I will be much more vigilant in the future. Not that this will preclude the possibility of unconsciously precipitating hurt, but I have taken on board the lessons learnt. It is through the grace of God that these situations can lead us to reconsider how we view painful experiences of the past.

In the previous chapter I alluded to a situation in which I was deeply wounded. This has been a profound source of learning for me, particularly in its juxtaposition with the later experience of being myself blamed for substantial damage to another person. I am revisiting it, in the hope that my own experience and recovery can act as pointers for others who may be in situations involving similar emotional upheavals, even though in quite different contexts.

The incident, as you will have gathered, took place many years ago, while I was still at school. I had been asked to fulfil a role, which I did to the best of my ability. But the way in which I performed this role did not fulfil the expectations of two people in authority. I was unaware of their dissatisfaction until they decided to demonstrate this publicly at the end of my term of office. They seem to have believed that I was an arrogant young upstart and were probably trying to teach me a lesson. But I was not who they thought I was – rather I was an extreme introvert determined to do my best without having to bother anyone. Their move shattered my self-confidence. And, as I mentioned in the previous chapter, it has taken me almost two decades to finally let this hurt go.

I believe that the two people concerned probably intended to take me down a peg or two, and such an action will always cause some pain. But I do not believe that they intended anything like the damage that they caused me. As I understand it now, they managed, inadvertently, to hit a fault-line in my psyche. We all have these veins of insecurity, generated as we grow up; I had masked mine by a coping strategy of appearing competent and self-sufficient. In one blow they shattered both of these things which left me feeling naked and defenceless. In many ways, I think now, it was the emotional equivalent of tripping someone, and by unfortunate coincidence dislocating their knee. For many years I held them accountable for the dislocation but I am able to see now that is not how it was.

What experiences do you have of forgiving, and what experiences do you have of being the one who needs to apologise?

When you think about an experience of conflict with someone, what happens if you imagine talking to this person in the presence of God?

Intention matters

The reason I have chosen to use this particular and very personal example is because it illustrates the point that the impact on the person wounded may well be far greater than the initial intent. It has made me reflect deeply on my experiences of being hurt, and it has enabled me to sit a little more lightly to some of the hurts I have experienced. And as I listen to others describing incidents in which they have been wronged in some way, the first question I find myself wanting to ask is: 'What do you think was the intent of the perpetrator?' This is the crucial question we have to ask ourselves when we realise that we have been seriously hurt.

In most ordinary relationships, between ordinary, healthy people who are trying to live ordinary good lives, when a problem arises that results in a hurting, this first wounding is probably not intentional. It may be selfish and thoughtless, but it is probably not intentional. When we feel wounded by someone it is crucial that we take time to consider the hurt, holding in our consciousness a presumption of the good will of this person: considering always that the cause may have been thoughtlessness rather than malice. Just as we would want others to do for us.

Pausing to reflect is also necessary in order to ascertain the appropriate response. Much of the unhappiness in our world exists because we often lash out as soon as we have been blindsided by hurt. The problem with this is that the hitting back does come with the intent to hurt, and very quickly we descend into a cascade of tit for tat – and then return to an equitable, loving space is well-nigh impossible. I think that this pause for reflection is what the gospels are calling for when they tell us to 'turn the other cheek'. It is not an instruction to remain in an abusive relationship, but rather an invitation to pause. If we pause long enough, and are able to communicate the hurt that we have experienced, and allow the other person to recognise the damage that they have caused, the escalation into intentional hurting can be avoided.

The manner in which we go about dealing with a hurt will depend on the quality and intensity of the relationship we have with that person. It can be a good idea to have an initial conversation with a third person – someone who is able to keep the conversation confidential; someone who cares deeply about us and who will give us the space to express our anger and hurt; someone who will not start accusing the person who caused the hurt. It is important too, to look carefully at our own behaviour to determine what, if anything, might have brought on the attack. This can help separate out the intensity of our own experience from the intention of the person who hurt us. A conversation with a third person will only be helpful if the person we speak to does not become affronted on our behalf – and actually add fuel to the fire.

Apology

But sometimes it is we who have precipitated the hurt. And then it is we who must initiate the healing. It is we who must apologise, and ask forgiveness.

Apology requires, first and foremost, an understanding and an admission that we ourselves were at fault. Real apology is not easy. It requires reflection, honesty and humility. It requires us to face the reality that we are not always at our best, that there are occasions when we operate from a space which is not only unedifying, but which can be distinctly destructive. Facing that in ourselves is not pleasant and it is not easy. Almost immediately we find self-justification emerging.

Whilst mitigating factors are important to consider, apology requires an admission that we have caused hurt – whether intentionally or not. For an apology to be effective, it also requires an understanding of the level of hurt experienced by the other. This is not to suggest that we are necessarily directly responsible for the full extent of the experience of hurt, as I have described above. Nonetheless, it is important that the one who caused the pain should understand and appreciate that, whatever their intent, the extent of damage experienced by the other may be far greater than they could have conceived. This requires we understand that our personal experience is only a part of the truth. Apology that fails to take cognisance of this difference will always be inadequate. The one apologising may find themselves defending their own intentions, and the one hurt may – rightly or wrongly, and whether they realise it or not – require an apology for the entire extent of the hurt. As a result, neither party will feel they have been understood. Under such circumstances, apology, however well intended, may not be seen to be adequate, and further communication may be necessary.

Forgiveness

For apology to have the desired effect, forgiveness must come in its wake. Forgiveness, at its best, will heal the forgiver as well as the one forgiven.

Even though forgiveness does not actually require the participation of the one who has done the hurting, it does demand genuine soul-searching by the forgiver. In my experience it requires the one forgiving to see the wounded, broken person who stands beyond the hurtful event that they have precipitated. Forgiveness requires an understanding of that person's limitations. But it also requires an understanding of our own brokenness and our own fault-lines. It requires that we see that our own reactions and responses may not be clear and unencumbered with baggage. It requires being able to see both the experience of our hurt and the intention of the other.

I strongly believe that the capacity to forgive is a grace. It is something we can work towards, by doing the necessary reflection; to try to see as much of the truth as we can. But this, while necessary, is not sufficient. A grace is something we can desire, but it is not attainable through hard work.

Grace is something we must ask for, something that we desire and which we continually pray for. And wait for; waiting on God. Sooner or later, we discover that the grace has been given. I have found that the experience of having forgiven someone usually takes me by surprise: I don't notice that I have managed to forgive until something external calls the hurtful situation to mind, and I realise that I am now viewing it differently.

The important thing to remember about forgiveness is that a lack of forgiveness is crippling to the soul. Holding on to the hurt – once it has been processed and set aside – by failing to forgive keeps all those involved bound to one another on some level. Forgiveness restores our interior freedom. The process of forgiving is almost impossible to define and it cannot be willed into existence. It is a grace. I have found that forgiveness brings a release in the depths of one's being.

Living with the aftermath

After an incident of hurting and feeling wounded, there is more than one way forward. What's best will be determined by the personalities involved, the nature of the harming act, and also by the surrounding situation – including who, if anyone, is at hand to help.

Reconciliation

Reconciliation is possible only if both forgiveness and apology are possible. That is to say, reconciliation is a product of being able to see beyond the current event, and, crucially, beyond our own experience of the event. It is necessary that both parties are able to do this, and that both parties see the relationship as worth continued investment. It also requires some communication about the event, and about the way forward.

Reconciliation requires, firstly, that an apology be offered and accepted. Secondly, forgiveness, even if it cannot be given immediately, must be present. Reconciliation is something that we live into once we have made the mutual decision to reconcile. Like forgiveness, it is also a grace to be prayed for, and it requires time.

Of course, by the time reconciliation is effected, there has usually been a bit of tit for tat. Indeed, the process of negotiating the distinctions between the hurt intended and the hurt experienced may be rather messy, and apology and forgiveness may be necessary on both sides.

Letting bygones be bygones

'Letting bygones be bygones' is quite different from reconciliation. It describes the scenario where it is clear that either apology or forgiveness or both are not currently possible (and indeed may never become possible). The reasons for this are usually around a lack of capacity to communicate the problem. At least one party may be simply unable or unwilling to see the situation from the other's perspective, or be unable or unwilling to take responsibility for their actions. Nevertheless, the relationship is such that walking away is not perceived to be a good choice. This is usually the case with conflict within families or in work relationships. Reconciliation may not be possible, but coexistence is still desirable – perhaps even necessary. Under these circumstances continued attempts at reconciliation may in fact be more destructive, at least in the short term.

It's easy to view 'letting bygones be bygones' as merely a poor cousin of reconciliation, but it is far more helpful to see it as a vast improvement on the alternative of never speaking again. The damaged relationship will probably remain strained and the people involved will not see each other as friends, but the relationship will probably be sufficiently robust for those concerned to be able to cope with family get-togethers or work situations. The choice here is to be polite and kind; to avoid talking about the past conflict in any way that adds fuel to fire, and to make sure that conversations are not masked attempts to draw others into the battle. When such a choice has been made, some ongoing support may be necessary for a while as we learn to live into the new dynamics. That support will probably have to come from people completely outside the conflictual situation, and we may even need to seek counsel to help us to deal with the problem.

Walking away

There are times when even letting bygones be bygones does not work. Then the best way forward is to walk away. These are usually associated with situations in which the breakdown of a relationship has had a large dimension of psychological transference or projection. Such relationships are characterised by an idealisation of one (or both) of the people involved, followed by an incident which destroys that illusion. The result is a backlash where the idealised person becomes hated instead of loved; despised instead of admired. If you are the person who has fallen from the pedestal there really is nothing you can do to aid the situation. Your continued interaction will probably be to the detriment of both of you in the long term. Having to walk away is not easy, but it is sometimes the most loving action.

Giving sufficient time

It is important in this healing process not to rush anything. There is a wonderful little book called *Don't Forgive Too Soon*[48] which points to the importance of taking the necessary time.

It takes time for the extent of the hurt to really settle in. It takes time to grasp that your actions have had an effect

---

48   Dennis Linn, Sheila Fabricant Linn and Matthew Linn (1997).

which you never intended – or to realise that your intended hurting was not a wise action. It takes time to communicate and to decide whether to move forward or not; to find a way to coexist or to truly reconcile. If we try to reconcile too quickly, the real lessons may not actually emerge, and we may find ourselves covering the same ground, having the same fights all over again.

Old wounds can get triggered inadvertently many years after we think we have laid them to rest. This can happen for at least two reasons. Firstly, because there is still a sensitivity in that area, or perhaps we do truly have a fault-line in that region. Secondly, because we have not quite done with the learning. The sign of an old wound being triggered is a massive overreaction to a new situation.

When old wounds are triggered we need to pause and pray as soon as we are able to. Perhaps the most useful way to begin the exploration of this space is to try to deal with ourselves compassionately. If we begin by berating ourselves for overreacting we are not likely to be able to engage in a way which will help lay the wounding to rest. One way to begin this exploration is to pause and notice how God is looking at us. It helps us get perspective, and it will make venturing back into the murky territory substantially easier as we are not alone – God is our companion. At this stage we may need to ask God to help us see what is truly a part of the current circumstance and what is our own baggage from the past. This is a process of discernment. Each time an old wounding is evoked there is usually something new to learn, and usually something to let go of. Praying for grace and wisdom is one of the most powerful ways to begin to disarm the internal landmine.

In conclusion

Dealing with problems in relationships is a messy business! More often than not, we come to full realisation that we are hurt only after we have struck back. Once retaliation has begun in earnest, it can spiral out of control very quickly and the causative event may become totally obscured. Then apology and forgiveness are very much mutual activities and the negotiation around who was hurt first, and who was hurt how much becomes far more complex. In intimate relationships there is also the tricky issue of the accumulation of little hurts that seem to have been allowed to slip by but which have not slipped anywhere at all, and are sitting front and centre as mini-cherry bombs to be lobbed back when required.

The healing of relationships is not simple, and I certainly do not write as one with great authority on this subject. I write as one who has held grudges for far too long and who has inadvertently caused substantial damage to someone else's life. I have no authority, except that I think the stark examples I have experienced have thrown the whole area into some kind of relief for me. This has given me the capacity to articulate what I see, even though I still navigate this landscape with difficulty. It has nevertheless also been one of the extraordinary privileges of my life to witness the grace of God working in this way in the lives of others.

Are there areas in your life where you need of the grace of being able to forgive?

Are there areas where you need to offer apology?

Are there little hurts that you have been storing up which you need to let of?

Do you have any fault-lines – areas which very often result in over-reaction?

Take some time to talk to God about any of these things.

Chapter 12: The Central Core

When prayer becomes an encounter with the living God, it becomes unpredictable. You thought you were doing something relatively safe – praying – and instead you find yourself face to face with someone real
— *Rob Marsh SJ*

The whole purpose of faith is to know God's presence right now, in and through whatever it is that we are doing. Someone commented to me that she has begun to realise that prayer is the essence of a life of faith – it is the thing which makes the difference, which allows for the development of real relationship with God. This was a woman who has been faithful in her church attendance and has belonged to a vibrant small group for years. It is not an uncommon experience; many people seem to think of prayer as 'one aspect' of faith life, rather than as the central core.

•••

For me, the central gift of Ignatian spirituality is that it is a spirituality for all people, in all circumstances. It requires nothing of us except that we pay attention to our thirst for God. As St Augustine put it – our souls are restless until they rest in God.

What impact does your faith have on your life? Where does relationship with God feature?

Paying attention

The invitation in Ignatian spirituality is to pay ever closer attention to that inner thirst. To notice what brings us peace, what brings us joy, what brings us a sense of God's presence. It is when we dare to notice the inner restlessness that we begin to recognise the difference between those things which truly bring us closer to God and the things which seem to hold promise, but which ultimately fail to deliver. We begin to notice the difference between eudaemonic desire and hedonic desire. We begin to notice the difference between intrinsic and extrinsic motivations.

The life of Christian faith is not about trying to get whatever the pass mark is in the test of life, so that we can sneak through the door of salvation. It is not about how many times we say the rosary, or how long it has been since we last went to confession (and yes herein I reveal my Roman Catholic heritage – other traditions will have other sorts of questions). No, the Christian journey is about companionship with Jesus. It is about living each day to the full. It is about growth and healing and transformation. It is not about fear of where we will ultimately end up. God is a loving God. Even more than that, God loves us unconditionally. Living the Christian life is not about securing salvation, it is about enjoying the presence of God in our lives right now, in the knowledge that it is the companionship of God which brings about transformation in our lives. We do not have to save ourselves; we do not have to change ourselves; all we need to do is invest in relationship with God. We need to allow God to love us and to allow ourselves to bask in that love. But in order to do that we need to learn to be honest with ourselves and with God. Love can only grow in a space which values honesty with God, and strives for honesty with God.

The more we come to recognise which things draw us towards God, and what pulls us away from God, the more we realise that we are broken. By that I mean that we begin to realise that many of the things that push us away from God are not external – rather they are a part of ourselves. They come from our own selfishness and our own ego defences. For the most part we have constructed those ego defences to protect ourselves. It is only as we begin to get a bit stronger in the balm of God's love that we realise that we no longer need to defend ourselves in that way. As soon as that happens, we begin to realise that it is the very mechanisms we have constructed to protect ourselves that so often cause damage to others. We realise that we ourselves are capable of destructive behaviour. And ultimately we realise that we cannot save ourselves: that we need the grace of God to navigate our daily reality.

For me, that recognition emerged on two particular occasions. The first was in 2002/3 as I contemplated the political situation in Zimbabwe. As I looked at the corruption and distortion of values I realised that the only thing that separated me from those who willingly participated in the process, was that I had not been exposed to those temptations. With that, I realised that I honestly do not know that I am any better than they are. I do not know that I am impervious to succumbing to similar temptations. It was a good lesson in humility; in understanding better Jesus's injunction: 'Judge not, that you be not judged'.

The second occasion occurred in 2010, when I came to recognise my own fundamental brokenness for the first time. To recognise that I had operated for far too long out of an energy which had its source in trying to prove some people wrong, trying to prove that I had value, trying to prove that I was worthy of being seen. But I have long since come to know that I do have value, and that operating out of that negative energy source meant that my actions and my being could be destructive to others. We cannot be part of the solution until we recognise that we are part of the problem. We cannot work for peace and reconciliation until we recognise the areas in ourselves which are still itching for a fight.

William Barry SJ, in his book *Changed Heart, Changed World*[49], writes:

> For too long in the history of Western Christian spirituality, repression of unwanted feelings, impulses, thoughts and desires was taught as the preferred method towards spiritual growth. But God wants us to heal through and through. To allow God to do this, we must be willing to face our darkest and most troubling impulses in God's healing presence.

One of the recurrent themes in this book has been the need for honesty. I really do believe that it is the only prerequisite which God asks of us. God does not need us to be good.

In her poem 'Wild Geese', Mary Oliver writes, 'You do not have to be good...You only have to let the soft animal of your body love what it loves[50].' If we can just dare to love, we will discover which things are truly important. We will be able to pick them out from among the myriad things crying out for our attention. It is essential to take time to be quiet, because some of the important things will only whisper gently to us.

Living life with hope

Irenaeus is attributed with saying, in the second century, that the glory of God is the human person fully alive. So how do we live to the full? Henry David Thoreau put it this way[51]:

> I went to the woods because I wished to live deliberately... and not, when I came to die, discover that I had

---

49   William Barry (2011) p.30.

50   Mary Oliver (2004) p.110.

51   Henry David Thoreau (1997) p. 66.

not lived... I wanted to live deep and suck out all the marrow of life... to put to rout all that was not life...

What does it mean, then, to 'live deliberately'? If we live in fear of 'getting it wrong', we will – if we are fortunate – discover that we have been missing out on the essence of life. We need to dare to love passionately. What I most love and value in Ignatian spirituality is that it is a spirituality which teaches us to deal with desire. Ignatius was not afraid of the chaos of daily life. Rather he was utterly convinced that God is present in all of it. If we can just bring ourselves to pause for long enough to notice, we will not be able to miss God's presence in our lives.

Living life with passion and with enthusiasm is no guarantee against loss or against pain. I have often found myself wondering why some people seem to have such a tough row to hoe whilst others seemingly swim through life unscathed. I do not know why this is, and contemplating the question doesn't seem to help me much. But I have come to know that, no matter what happens and however tough it gets, God really is in the midst of the chaos. If Jesus had the courage to go through his Passion, what tribulation of ours would he shy away from? He was rejected by those he was trying to help, denied by his closest companions and put through unimaginable torture. When we are having a tough time, he is right there in the midst of it. We are not alone. It may be scary and it may be overwhelmingly painful, but we are not alone. In God, in the mystery of Easter, we have the promise of redemption. We have the promise of resurrection.

We do not know what the next world will look like. I find the concept of salvation as being a gateway to the next world a little abstract – and I am a bit too pragmatic to live my life by that kind of idea. What will happen in the world to come will take care of itself. Rather, I put my faith in redemption because I have seen it happen in my own life. I have seen the unbelievable healing power of God at work in my own soul. There have been three or four occasions in my adult life

191

where I have looked back and wondered what on earth happened. How did that place of pain grow into this place of joy?

In the Fourth Week of the Spiritual Exercises, as you contemplate the resurrection, the grace to be prayed for is joy with Christ in joy. The joy here is far more than a 'happiness' or 'contentment' – it is a deep sense of well-being. Things can still be messy; the Resurrection was hardly a return to 'business as usual' for the disciples. But in the very depths of your being is a visceral echo of the oft-repeated phrase of Julian of Norwich 'All will be well, and all will be well, and all manner of things will be well'.

That said, I should mention that joy always takes me slightly by surprise – as though it had been slowly taking root and growing for a while before I noticed it.

> When I stop to examine my spirit
> I discover that it is not as I thought it was.
> As I bend to grasp the dry brittle sponge
> I find it is heavy and laden with water.
> Not just laden, but saturated.
> I had not noticed the Spirit's gentle soaking;
> too busy straining to hear the sound
> I did not notice my spirit soak up
> the life giving force.
> As I scanned the horizon for rain clouds
> I failed to notice the tiny stream.
> How often, Lord, how often do I lament,
> cry out in frustration
> that I lack what others have
> and yet on pausing to examine myself
> I discover I have more than I dared dream.
> The eternal becoming is true blessing[52].

The times of suffering in our lives can often have a sharp edge to them – a clear cause and a distinct before and af-

---

52   Margaret Blackie (2008) p.96.

ter. But the emergence of joy is often far more subtle. We do not really notice that things have changed until something catches our attention. The dry, brittle sponge of struggle is actually infused with joy – we just haven't quite realised it. I think this happens partly because we have a specific idea of how things are 'supposed' to be, or perhaps because we have become accustomed to our role as sufferer. When things don't appear in the guise we expect them to, we can easily overlook them. The emergence of joy is no different. It takes us by surprise because it is rarely packaged in the way we expect.

Whilst I believe that joy is a grace – something to be prayed for, rather than something that can be achieved through the force of will – it is worth reminding ourselves yet again that we can help ourselves along the way by making use of discernment.

Ignatius offers us the simple tools of discernment: notice those things which draw you closer to God and those things which pull you further away from God. Notice those things which help you to move towards greater authenticity and greater personal integration, and those things which you would rather keep hidden and which lead to fragmentation. Notice those things which lead to deeper relationships and those which foster shallow, passing acquaintance. Give time, space and energy to those things which enrich relationship with God, which foster authenticity and which deepen relationships. Set aside those things which do not. Know that as you practise discernment, you will uncover areas of unfreedom, areas of brokenness, and areas of woundedness. Know too, that God is with you, and God wants to heal you. Healing does not mean that the wounds will disappear, but rather that through the grace of God you will come to see that the wounding is not something to be ashamed of, but rather it is the seedbed of compassion and wisdom.

Do not misunderstand me – do not go and look for pain! When you have joy – savour it. Trust that it is God's will and desire that you should live life to the full; that you should love passionately. The new heaven and new earth promised to us do not come at the expense of anyone. We can choose to engage fully and deliberately, trusting that when we get it wrong we can ask for forgiveness, and find a new route. Failing to risk loving, failing to risk living, is failing to answer the one true call that we have – to be fully ourselves. Denise Ackermann is a well known South African theologian and a good friend of mine. She always says that the question she believes that she will have to answer at the end of her life is: 'Did you have the courage to be Denise?' It is a powerful question. Do you have the courage to love? Do you have the courage to use your talents? Do you have the courage to acknowledge your brokenness? Do you have the courage to live *your* life to the full? Gerard Manley Hopkins expresses a similar idea in this section from his poem 'As kingfishers catch fire':

> Each mortal thing does one thing and the same:
> Deals out that being indoors each one dwells;
> Selves – goes itself; *myself* it speaks and spells,
> Crying *Whát I dó is me: for that I came.*

Once again we return to the theme of honesty. There is only one thing worth committing to in the spiritual journey and that is to be as honest as we can be – with ourselves, and with God. Of course honesty requires that we pay attention to the feedback we are getting from the world around us too. We are likely to trip up along the way. We may fail to follow through on our commitment. We may miss praying; we may break a promise; we may hurt a person we truly love – we will commit countless sins. What we need to do here is to 'own' these failings, to bring them before God, and to trust in the grace of forgiveness.

It is not easy to commit to honesty. It can be very scary. We are forced to face the best and the worst in ourselves. But nothing short of honesty will give us entry to the life we dare to hope for.

What does living a life of faith mean to you?
Where do you place your hope?
Take time to talk to God about these things.

Chapter 13: Looking Forward

What I do is me: for that I came
— Gerard Manley Hopkins

A t the end of a retreat it is normal for the spiritual director to ask the retreatant to spend some time 'gathering
the fruit'. This chapter serves something of the same purpose.

• •

Having read thus far, and clearly beginning to close in on the end of
the book, what stays with you?

Which ideas have been significant?

Has there been anything that has helped you to see things in a new
light?

Is there any change that you want to make in your daily practice?

Many years ago a family friend made the observation that
most of us overestimate what we can achieve in a year and
underestimate what we can achieve in a decade. I have heard
the same observation in different guises over the years since,
and it is always a useful reminder to me. The simple point:
do not expect big changes too quickly, but dare to hope for a
seismic shift over time.

I have been most blessed in having stumbled into Ignatian
spirituality and made the Spiritual Exercises in my early
twenties. The discipline of prayer instilled in those years has

stuck. This, coupled with the fact that I am a morning person, and am naturally both introverted and reflective, allowed me to take to a routine of daily prayer like a duck to water and it has remained with me into my late thirties. No doubt the absence of children or a significant other in my life has made it relatively easy for me to continue this routine. Nonetheless, I have been reflecting in recent months on just how far I have come in the spiritual journey. It feels as though the discipline of the last fifteen years is really beginning to bear fruit. It is not that my experience of God now is more visceral or more tangible; rather I am beginning to see the fruit manifest in my being. I am beginning to see that I do approach the challenges of daily life a little differently from the way many of my contemporaries do. I have found easy companionship and have gained the respect of people who are twice my age. But most importantly, I am happy in my own skin. I am delighted with the life I have managed to create for myself and I am enormously grateful for the quality of relationship that I enjoy with a variety of people. I believe all of that has come from a growing willingness to be honest with myself about where I am and what I am struggling with.

Repetition

In *The Spiritual Exercises* there is a kind of prayer called 'repetition'. In the thirty-day retreat, the exercitant is given two or three different scripture passages or exercises to pray with. In a standard day, the exercitant makes five prayer periods. The fourth and fifth prayer periods are repetitions. As with the term 'indifference', the English word does not really capture the intended Ignatian meaning. Repetition is not a process of trying to recreate or recapture an earlier prayer period. Rather it is an invitation to return to those times of consolation where encounter with God was most tangible, and to allow God to take one deeper into the experience. It requires a little bit of reflection, noticing where God has seemed most present, and *an active choosing to return to those times*, allowing God to take one a bit further, allowing God to come a bit closer.

In a similar way, much of what you will read in this section has been present in earlier chapters. It is a reminder of what has gone before and an invitation to pick up one or maybe two of the suggestions which resonated most with you. It is very easy in reading this kind of book to move a little too quickly from one section to the next and in that way some of the seeds are not planted quite as well as they might have been. It is my hope then that this section will serve as a gentle encouragement to continue what you are already doing. Do not feel that it is necessary to add something to your spiritual practice unless you feel a real draw to do so. It may not be the time.

The practice of gratitude

In October 2011 I watched a talk by Matt Cutts on TED.com entitled 'Try something new for thirty days'. Given that it had been quite a challenging year, I decided that I would post one thing that I was grateful for on my Facebook page every day for thirty days. It was a very useful exercise. Not only to think about what I was most grateful for each day, but to articulate that and share it. I found pretty quickly that several friends joined me in the challenge, and months after I had stopped posting the notes people would comment on how useful they had found it themselves, even though they hadn't participated online. I repeated the process for Lent 2012. The combination of the two chunks of time where I consciously focused on gratitude has facilitated an internal shift. I *am* more grateful. I am sure I can continue to grow in this capacity and I intend to continue to focus on this aspect. Being more grateful – more consciously grateful – means I cannot help but be aware of the gifts and blessings in my life.

Praying for the grace

This is such a simple idea, but can be a little difficult to put into practice. Praying for the grace requires paying attention to where you are in your being. It requires noticing the challenges and difficulties you face and being as honest as you can be about this, and then offering this poverty of spirit to God, asking God for the grace to move through whatever this difficulty is. Often this will require a willingness to let go of something. The challenge here is the willingness to see things as they really are. The turbulent time my family was experiencing when I was living in France was enormously challenging for me, not only because of the sense of isolation, but also because it caused me to question my faith. My dad had taken a stand for justice, and it had ended up costing a great deal. I found it very difficult to reconcile my idea of God being a God of justice and a God who cares, with the fact that things were turning out very badly for my family. I barely spoke French, and I had no friends in the area. Nevertheless, when I read over my journals from that time, there is a sense of willed positivity which does not correlate with my memory of my experience. I think I was afraid of being honest in my prayer. I was afraid of where that honesty would lead me. There was certainly no mention in my journals of the fundamental questioning about the very existence of God that was taking place within me – until I had discovered once more that I did actually believe.

In recent years I have learnt the power of being honest about my fears or about the pain that I am experiencing. I have found that, rather than consuming me, allowing myself to own the feeling has enabled me to name the grace that I need. And in praying for the grace over a period of time, I find something begins to shift. My recovery time is much better, and I don't find myself going over the same material months later, trying to reconcile it once again.

I am well aware that this idea of 'owning where I am today' is somewhat contrary to the widely popular idea that our thoughts define our reality. This attitude is most apparent in books like Rhonda Byrne's best-selling *The Secret*[53], where the power of positive thinking is presumed to be the recipe for a happy life. My own experience has been of times of 'stuckness' that I cannot simply will myself out of. For me, the combination of leaning into the rawness of the experience and praying for the grace that I need is what facilitates internal shifts. Through my daring to sit in the truth of my experience, real healing occurs, rather than a papering over of the problem. I think my appreciation for my life has grown substantially as a direct result: I am not waiting for my dreams to come true one day, I am living a life that I love today, and I am proud of the way in which I have been able to navigate the past few years.

Holistic living

A healthy spiritual life is built on more than simply good spiritual practice. Mental, emotional and physical wellbeing also play a role. Just as building relationship with God requires development in relationships with self and others, so too, spiritual growth demands care for one's mental, emotional and physical being. This is not to say that one needs to be healthy for growth to occur, but rather that care for the soul will sooner or later require a growth in attention towards and care of one's whole being.

It is inevitable that sooner or later some traumatic event will occur in one's life – whether this is an acute trauma such as a sudden death, a job loss, physical injury or violent crime, or a more chronic problem. Since the identification of the condition known as post-traumatic stress disorder, there has been a great deal of research into the effects of trauma on individuals. This has revealed that many individuals experience tremendous growth following a traumatic event. This has been dubbed 'post-traumatic growth'. One of the ways to promote

53   Rhonda Byrne (2007).

post-traumatic growth is to develop mental, emotional, physical and social resilience in times of strength and calm. Each of these different aspects of resilience promotes growth and increases one's capacity to respond to trauma. But a desire to generate resilience doesn't arrive magically following a trauma. Rather, the resilience we have built up over time gives us the capacity to deal with trauma in a growth-generating way once the initial period of paralysis has begun to shift. A healthy spiritual life, then, is also aided by paying attention to those aspects which help generate resilience.

Spiritual direction

I find spiritual direction enormously helpful. I have had a spiritual director for most of my adult life. Spiritual direction is a conversation which bears some resemblance to most forms of talk therapy in that the one going for spiritual direction will self-disclose to a far greater degree than the spiritual director. But it is distinct from conventional therapy in that it is not a conversation about God, it is a conversation which facilitates encounter with God. The purpose of spiritual direction is deepening relationship with God. The main tool of spiritual direction is discernment, and the process of spiritual direction increases our ability to discern. I have found that having a good spiritual director has been a wonderful aid. Both in times of immense gratitude and in times of confusion, pain and upset, it has been a real gift to me.

Until recently I found it quite difficult to trust the people in my life to step up and help me out when I was struggling with something, but I have long been able to trust my spiritual directors. Many years ago I used to go to a very gentle, wise Jesuit priest. I remember thinking that I could say anything to him and he was never visibly shocked. Having practised as a spiritual director myself for almost a decade, I now know the importance of simply listening to a person's story and helping them to find God in that story, regardless of its content. In the beginning, spiritual direction aided me in the development of the discipline of prayer. Having to have a conversation about what was going on in my spiritual life required that I begin to take it seriously, and that I pay attention to what is happening. Even with spiritual directors who have been adequate but not excellent, the process of trying to articulate what is going on inside me helps me clarify nebulous feelings, and results in the crystallisation of thoughts and ideas – and deepens my encounter with God. Over time I have come to value the support of spiritual direction in both calm and stormy times. It provides a place of accountability and a place of caring trust in which the director and I both seek to see and to savour the action of God in my life.

Everyday choices

The small everyday choices really matter. Attitude is both a choice and a habit and it does not necessarily have much to do with external circumstances. In reading Ingrid Betancourt's account of her six years in captivity in the Columbian jungle, *Even Silence Has an End*, I was struck by this paragraph:

> I, too, could choose how to react. But I was often wrong. Life in captivity had not removed the necessity to act in the right way. It was not about pleasing others or gaining support. I felt I had to change. Rather than try to adapt to the ignominy of the situation, I had to learn to be a better person[54].

This single, crucial paragraph captures the essence of the attitude which allowed her experience to become profoundly transformative rather than destructive. It is this recognition that, even in those circumstances, where she has to ask permission, for example, to go to the toilet area, there are still important life-shaping choices to be made.

---

54   Ingrid Betancourt (2010) p.175.

Most of us beyond our mid thirties have made choices which somehow fix our lives. It may be a particular career path, a marriage, having children, buying property. Inevitably in these spaces there will be times of great challenge. And all the way along we have to pay attention to the manner in which we are choosing to respond. At this point you may be saying to yourself: 'But you don't really understand; it's different for me.' A few years ago, I was trying to decide where I should be and what I should be doing. I was doing a postdoc at the time and was considering going across to Boston with a view to working in the pharmaceutical industry. I felt incredibly trapped by my circumstances. Now, as I look back I find it hard to see quite what I felt trapped by, but I know that I felt trapped and I suspect it was partly due to my own expectations of myself. One afternoon while I was at the gym it occurred to me that I had never been unemployed and I have never taken a job that I did not believe wholeheartedly was the right thing for me to be doing. At that point I realised that the sense of being trapped had been in my head; it was not real. My perspective shifted and with that the sense of being trapped disappeared precisely because the sense of being trapped was a mental construction not a reality. So let me say again: all the way along we need to pay attention to how we are responding.

Contrary to the ideas advocated in some popular literature, I do not believe we can completely create our own realities. Real world circumstances are not trivial, but, whatever our real circumstances may be, we do have a choice in how we navigate through the day. I am constantly amazed at how some of the small things I find myself thinking or feeling or doing can reveal an unhealthy attitude in some particular aspect of my life. When I see it, I am able to change it, and almost immediately I feel better about whatever it is. For example, shortly before I read the chapter of *Even Silence Has an End* which contains the paragraph quoted above, I had been grappling with my resistance to giving a talk at a chemistry conference. I had been gently fantasising about what serious illness I could fake which would prevent me from going to the conference. (Not my finest hour!) But when I read that paragraph I had a wakeup call. I could resist giving the talk and have a miserable week. Or I could throw myself into it and give it my best shot. Regardless of the outcome of the talk (okay, it went well), I felt better because I had faced the issue and dealt with it head on.

The practice of noticing

All the suggestions I have made thus far are ones that have been proven useful to people in various walks of life. Sometimes life circumstances will make finding a chunk of time for daily prayer very difficult, or the absence of a good spiritual director in your area may make spiritual direction impossible. But the practice of paying attention to where you are emotionally, spiritually and physically is always possible for all of us. This, coupled with the conscious noticing of where God is, and of 'how is God looking at me', is the Ignatian bedrock of a life of faith. Faith in this sense is not an allegiance to a particular set of doctrinal statements, it is a lived reality. Noticing the dynamics present in the moment will allow for a much more conscious engagement in life. And the inclusion of the noticing of God in the process opens the door to experiencing God's active engagement in the minutiae of our lives. Not necessarily in the sense of God answering our prayers, but in the sense – again – of development of relationship with God.

Finally...

Notice, as you come to the end of this chapter, what remains with you.

Have you made any resolutions?

Are there some ideas which you want to hold onto?

Have you enjoyed reading this book? If so, why?

The educator in me is very aware that this book will have little impact unless the ideas it contains are carried into conversation, and the practices it puts forward are actually integrated into daily life.

If there has been anything in these pages that has resonated deeply with you, take time to notice it, acknowledge it, and give thanks to God for it. Find a way that is appropriate to remind yourself of it every day for the next thirty days. If it is an idea, and if you can, talk about it, explain it to others. If it is a way of praying or some kind of spiritual practice, then make sure you allot yourself time to try it.

Principle and Foundation

The goal of our life is to live with God forever.
God, who loves us, gave us life.
Our own response of love allows God's life
to flow into us without limit.
All the things in this world are a gift of God,
presented to us so that we can know God more easily
and make a return of love more readily.
As a result, we appreciate and use all these gifts of God
insofar as they help us develop as loving persons.
But if any of these gifts become the center of our lives,
they displace God
and so hinder our growth toward our goal.
In everyday life, then, we must hold ourselves in balance
before all of these created gifts insofar as we have a choice
and are not bound by some obligation.
We should not fix our desires on health or sickness,
wealth or poverty, success or failure, a long life or a short one.
For everything has the potential of calling forth in us
a deeper response to our life in God.
Our only desire and our one choice should be this:
I want and choose what better leads
to God's deepening his life in me. [55]

Notice what strikes you this time.

Notice whether anything has shifted in you in reading this book. Maybe nothing has changed but some things have crystallised or clarified.

Take time to talk to God a little about these things.

---

55   David Fleming (1993) p.9.

Epilogue

*Take Lord, receive, all my liberty, my understanding and my
entire will, all that I have and possess. You give it all to me;
to you I return it. All is yours, dispose of it entirely
according to your will. Give me only your love
and your grace for that is enough for me.*

This powerful, arresting prayer is the culmination of *The
Spiritual Exercises*[56]. Over time this prayer has meant many
things to me. In the beginning, it was a prayer that I hoped I
would one day have the courage to pray. Even as I prayed it at
that time I had very clear ideas of what it meant to give my
liberty, my understanding and my will to God. Many years
on, I continue to pray this prayer with some trepidation. The
first part still catches me a little because I know that if I dare
to be honest with myself I find yet more of myself to which
I still cling tightly. There is a tension in me between the ongoing desire for freedom and the ongoing fear of what that
freedom will actually cost. But now that I have truly begun
to explore the dynamic of grace, I begin to glimpse the truth
of the final sentence of the prayer. If I do have God's love
and God's grace, I have everything I need. Perhaps not everything I seem to want, but everything I need.

In a very real way, understanding the dynamic of grace quells
the fear of surrender implied in the first few lines of the
prayer. Grace is a remarkable phenomenon. In one sense we
are held in existence by the grace of God, and so there is no
way to escape God's grace. But our capacity to touch and experience that grace is limited by our desire for control; our
desire to dictate the way in which things will turn out; and

---

56   Michael Ivens (2006) [234].

our lack of freedom – of indifference – regarding the outcome of a particular experience. Grace, in my internal glossary, speaks of an experience of consciously giving something over God, in the awareness that I do not quite know what the outcome is going to be. Praying for a particular grace is, for me, an act of surrender. It is an acknowledgement of my own limitations, of the unfreedoms I have discovered in myself; and it is a willingness to let God take me where God wills.

To put it a slightly different way, praying for a grace is, for me, an act of faith. It contains an act of contrition, or at least an acknowledgement of my own weakness. I am usually only able to pray for grace once I have seen my own sense of attachment to a particular outcome, and with that usually comes a sense of my own shortcomings or weaknesses. It also contains an element of praise. This may not be expressed directly, but handing over a desire to God, for God to do with what God wills, is impossible without a real experiential understanding that God is *for* me in a very fundamental sense. Ultimately God desires that which will be best for me in the grand scheme of things. That bigger picture may require some loss or letting go. Certainly it contains an element of surrender or trust. It requires that I hand over whatever it is to God, and that I allow God to be God. This requires honesty with myself and honesty before God.

Ultimately, a prayer for grace is always answered. Part of the process of this way of praying is learning a new way of being in the world. All manner of things *will* be well, and there will be joy, even though it may not look quite the way you hoped for when you began praying. Part of the process of praying for grace is a strange mix of letting go of expectations whilst continuing to be present to one's desires. It is a willingness to see the truth and to wrestle with that truth, however ugly and painful it may be. Interior freedom is built on honesty.

This way of praying also increases our humility. It is impossible to sit with our own attachments, our own sense of weakness, and our own failings without recognising that, however far along the path to enlightenment we may think we are, we really have not got there at all. We may have grown enormously, we may celebrate significant parts of ourselves as being transformed, but in the end there is always more to be done.

The spiritual journey is not about attaining perfection, it is about connecting with God. Prayer is not an activity so much as it is a way of life.

Take Lord, receive, all my liberty, my understanding and my entire will, all that I have and possess. You give it all to me; to you I return it. All is yours, dispose of it entirely according to your will. Give me only your love and your grace for that is enough for me.

Glossary

Note: these words are defined here in terms of the way they are used in the context of this book.

Ascetic: A form of religious practice characterised by extreme self-discipline and abstention from all forms of indulgence.

Apophatic: This is a theological standpoint which actively avoids the use of words, images or metaphors in order to understand the nature of God – because these can never be adequate to describe the nature of God (compare with cataphatic).

Cataphatic: This is a theological standpoint which uses words, images and metaphors in order to understand the nature of God (compare with apophatic).

Colloquy: In the Ignatian usage this is a conversation in prayer, usually between yourself and Jesus, but it can be extended to the other members of the Trinity, or to Mary or one of the saints.

Consolation: In Ignatian usage this refers to an internal orientation which is aligned with God. It involves those things which facilitate deepening relationship with God. Although consolation is usually characterised by feelings of well-being, painful consolation is also possible.

Desolation: In Ignatian usage this refers to an internal orientation which is out of alignment with God. It involves those things which inhibit deepening relationship with God. Desolation should not be confused with depression.

Discernment: The process whereby we prayerfully separate the wheat from the chaff of our daily experience, noticing and choosing those things which seem to be drawing us closer to God and gently setting aside those things which seem to be pulling us away from God.

Disordered desire: In Ignatian terms this is any desire which is placed above the desire for deeper relationship with God. The desire itself may be good and noble, but if placed above the desire for God it will ultimately lead you away from God.

Emotional granularity: The capacity to distinguish between closely related feelings.

Eudaemonic desire: A desire that is motivated primarily by seeking meaning and purpose (compare with hedonic desire).

Examen: This is a short prayer usually done at the end of the day. The purpose is to focus your attention on areas of your day where you have been most aware of God's presence or activity, and those times when you have been least aware of God's presence and activity. You then take time to talk to God about what you have noticed.

Exercitant: A person who is making the Spiritual Exercises of St Ignatius of Loyola.

Extrinsic motivation: Motivation which exists only in the presence of external rewards or recognition

Granularity: See Emotional granularity.

Hedonic desire: A desire that is motivated primarily by seeking pleasure (compare with eudaemonic desire).

Imaginative contemplation: A form of prayer associated with cataphatic spirituality in which you use your imagination as a vehicle for prayer. The classic form is to take a scene from a Gospel and to imagine that you are a part of the scene. It usually ends with a conversation with Jesus.

Indifference: In Ignatian usage this is the internal disposition where you are able to surrender to God your hopes, desires or fears for a particular outcome, trusting that in God all will be well. It should not be confused with the everyday meaning of this word.

Intrinsic motivation: Motivation which is satisfied by your own sense of purpose.

Lectio divina: This is the term given to prayerful reflection on a passage of Scripture.

Mimetic desire: A desire which emerges because you see someone else enjoying something.

Movement of spirits: Ignatius uses the term 'spirits' to encompass the internal result of any kind of internal or external stimulus which causes an internal disturbance. That disturbance in your inner being is a movement.

Repetition: Revisiting an experience from a previous prayer period in order that God might take you a little deeper into the experience, or that you come to a greater understanding of your relationship with God.

Retreat: This can take several forms. In the Ignatian tradition it is usually a period of time (anything from a weekend to thirty days) in which you undertake to be silent, to refrain from any contact with the outside world (no phones, no social media, no newspapers, no internet). Reading is usually prohibited, or at least substantially reduced. There are two major forms of retreat – the preached retreat, where one retreat leader gives talks to a group of people and provides points for prayer, and the individually guided retreat, where the retreatant has a private conversation with a spiritual director each day. (See also next entry.)

Retreat in daily life: This phrase is used in slightly different ways in various parts of the world. Generally it can be taken to mean a period time – short or long – during which one sees a spiritual director about once week, and commits to praying each day, for perhaps half an hour, over that period. It is sometimes used specifically to refer to making the full Spiritual Exercises in everyday life (this form is also called the 19th Annotation Retreat).

Reflective rumination: The process of gently reflecting on your experience over some time period, to fully understand the dynamics of what has happened in order to learn from the experience.

Ruminative brooding: A self-absorbed internal dialogue which results in cementing your sense of self-righteousness.

Spirits: This is a broad term, encompassing any thought, feeling, emotion, desire and so on, which moves us. A 'spirit' may be internal or external in origin. A 'good spirit' is one which inclines us towards God, and a 'bad spirit' is one which inclines us towards 'the enemy of our human nature'. Spirits may be supernatural in origin, but may also be simply the result of psychological processes.

Spiritual direction: This is defined by Barry and Connolly[57] as 'help given by one believer to another that helps the latter to pay attention to God's personal communication to him or her, to respond to this personally communicating God, to grow in intimacy with this God, and to live out the consequences of the relationship'.

Theodicy: Theological arguments developed for the purpose of trying to explain how suffering and evil can exist if God is a loving God.

---

57   William A Barry and William J Connolly (2012) p.6.

References

George Aschenbrenner (2007) *Consciousness Examen*. Loyola Press: Chicago, IL.

Gil Bailie (1999) 'René Girard's Contribution to the Church of the 21st Century', *Communio: International Catholic Review*, 26 No. 1 (Spring): 134–153.

William Barry SJ (2011) *Changed Heart, Changed World: The transforming freedom of friendship with God*. Loyola Press: Chicago, IL.

William A Barry SJ and William J Connolly SJ (2012) *The Practice of Spiritual Direction*. HarperOne: New York, NY.

Ingrid Betancourt (2010) *Even Silence Has an End: My Six Years of Captivity in the Columbian Jungle*. Penguin Press: New York, NY.

Margaret Blackie (2008) *Through the Unknown Remembered Gate*. New Voices Publishing: Cape Town.

Brené Brown (2010) *The Gifts of Imperfection*. Hazelden: Center City, MN.

Brené Brown (2012) *Daring Greatly*. Gotham Books: New York, NY.

Rhonda Byrne (2007) *The Secret*. Atria Books/Beyond Words: New York, NY.

Sheila Cassidy (1982) *Prayer for Pilgrims*. Crossroads Publishing Company: New York, NY.

Joan Chittister (2012) *Following the Path: The Search for a life of passion, purpose and joy*. Random House Digital: New York, NY.

TS Eliot (1974) *Collected Poems 1909–1962*. Faber and Faber: London.

David Fleming (1993) 'Soul of Christ', in Michael Harter SJ (ed.) *Hearts on Fire – Praying with Jesuits*. Institute for Jesuit Sources, St Louis, MI.

David Fleming (1996) *Draw me into your Friendship: The Spiritual Exercises – a literal reading and a contemporary translation*. Institute of Jesuit Sources, St Louis, MO.

Victor Frankl (2006) *Man's Search for Meaning*. Beacon Press: Boston.

George Ganss, SJ (1992) *The Spiritual Exercises of St Ignatius of Loyola. A translation and Commentary* (orig c.1548). Loyola Press: Chicago IL.

Gerard W Hughes (1996) *God of Surprises*. Darton, Longman & Todd: London.

Michael Ivens (2006) *The Spiritual Exercises of St Ignatius of Loyola* (translation). Gracewing: Leominster, UK.

Stephen Joseph (2011) *What Doesn't Kill Us: the new psychology of posttraumatic growth*. Basic Books: New York, NY.

Dennis Linn, Sheila Fabricant Linn and Matthew Linn (1997) *Don't Forgive Too Soon*. Paulist Press: Mahwah, NJ.

Ivan Mann (2005) *Breathing, I Pray*. Darton, Longman & Todd: London.

Mary Oliver (2004) *New and Selected Poems, Volume 1*. Beacon Press: Boston, MA.

Mary Oliver (2012) *House of Light*. Beacon Press: Boston, MA.

Karl Rahner (2004) *Karl Rahner: Spiritual Writings* (ed. Philip Endean). Orbis Books: Maryknoll, NY.

Dorothy Sayers (1974) 'Why Work?' In *Creed or Chaos*? (orig. c.1942) Sophia Institute Press: Manchester, NH.

Margaret Silf (2012) *Just call me López*. Loyola Press: Chicago, IL.

Philip T Starks (2012) *The Andovers*, November.

Henry David Thoreau (1997) *Walden* (orig. 1854). Oxford University Press: Oxford.

Michele Tugade, Barbara Fredrickson and Lisa Feldman Barrett (2004) 'Psychological Resilience and Positive Emotional Granularity', *Journal of Personality*: 72(6), 1161–1190.

Bronnie Ware (2012) *The Top Five Regrets of the Dying: A Life Transformed by the Dearly Departing*. Hay House: Carlsbad, CA.

Made in the USA
Middletown, DE
31 August 2015